Silly Things Atheists Believe: A Soul Winner's Guide to Atheists' Minds

Jeff A. Payne

Seminary Press

Published in the United States of America
by Seminary Press - Beaumont, TX

A personal and wholly-owned imprint of Pastor Jeff Payne

Library of Congress Cataloging-in-publication data.

Payne, Jeff A.
Silly Things Atheists Believe: A Soul-winners Guide to Atheists' Minds

ISBN: 9798359959520

DEDICATION

To my sweet, compassionate, honest, godly, and beautiful Kathleen:
Thanks for your tireless input, feedback, and love. You are always the
sunshine of my life, right after Jesus, but before any and everything else.

CONTENTS

ACKNOWLEDGMENTS

These acknowledgments are, of course, obligatory, but they are more than that. I am genuinely grateful for many people who covered for me, and took up the slack I left, while I wrote this book. First, of course, all glory and honor belong to the Lord Jesus, Who alone is worthy of all praise.

Kathleen kept stopping important and pressing work to listen to every new way I decided to phrase some concept, chapter, or paragraph. Tanner Howell had to preach more than his fair share, and we loved it. Billy Ray Harper preached for me, stayed "closer than a brother," and always had my back in his prayer closet. Doug Taylor remained a helpful and intimidating professor/mentor, the thought of whom helped me push through to completion.

My ministry mentors include David Brett, Ralph Burrage, Scott Camp, Bobby Cooksey, John Cope, Jay Dennis, Jerry Falwell, Jerry Field, Ronnie Floyd, Mike Harmon, Billy Harper, Herschel Hobbs, Richard Hogue, Don Jones, Craig Miller, Ernie Perkins, Larry Perkins, Kevin Phillips, John Powers, Dan Reid, Bob Rowley, Shawn Smith, Russ Tyler, and my dear parents, Robert Payne, and JoAnne Yeargan.

Introduction

If you're an atheist, I did not write this book for you, so please keep any complaints to yourself. Whether you agree or disagree with my assessments, I am stating how I see things. I have been interacting with atheists and agnostics for many decades, and I am in the best position to know what I perceive to be true and accurate – i.e., to proffer my *informed*, but *personal* opinions. Just as atheists may talk about theists with one another in ways that would be too condescending and uncivil to repeat in their presence, in this book we are having an in-house (Christian) discussion about atheists. Just like no two theists are alike, however, neither are any two atheists. [Atheist reader, I do not think you are "silly," not in the least, but I am characterizing some of the things you believe as "silly," at least from my perspective. I am sure you feel the same way about some of my beliefs, so try not to be *too* hypocritical in your reactions.]

Most atheists prefer to be defined as someone who simply lacks a belief in God. Yet, if that was *all* they were saying, there would not be much to talk about, as it is all but impossible, in this forum, to do a detailed report on the psychological state of a wide variety of people who call themselves atheists. But, as Professor John Lennox states so well, atheism is more than a statement about what is in someone's head:

> You cannot deny the existence of God without asserting a whole raft of beliefs about the nature of the world. That is why Richard Dawkins' book *The God Delusion* is not just a one-page tract stating that he doesn't believe in God. It is a lengthy volume dedicated to his atheistic worldview, naturalism, which holds that the universe/multiverse is all that exists, that what scientists call "mass energy" is the fundamental stuff of the universe, and that there is nothing else.[1]

All the core beliefs of atheism may be investigated. They are either true or false, or at least more plausibly true or false. Either we live in a theistic universe, or we do not. If we do, then it is not those who believe in God that are delusional, but quite the other way around.

To my core audience, why a book on the silly ideas atheists hold? There are three reasons: First, Christians who have not studied atheism, do not speak to atheists often, or are not trained in philosophy

---

[1] John Lennox, *Can Science Explain Everything?* (Charlotte, NC: The Good Book Co., 2019), 17.

are often intimidated by arguments from atheists that are frankly a bit silly. Being armed with how and why many atheists are not thinking clearly may help Christians converse with them in more meaningful and productive ways. Second, there are plenty of books written every year that touch on these misconceptions, but not many small-group curriculums deal with these matters on a popular, but still scholarly level. I felt there was a gap in the current offerings, or I would have simply pointed people to the existing material. Finally, to be fair, there are also numerous ways in which (many) Christians are also not thinking clearly – using circular reasoning (the Bible is true because it says it is), arguments from authority (my position is true because some famous preacher agrees with me), straw man arguments (arguing against things their opponents are not asserting) and numerous other logical fallacies (arguing logically incoherent claims).

This book is organized into thirteen chapters so that small groups can use it as a thirteen-week curriculum. At the end of each chapter are discussion starters, questions, and/or group activities designed to help people in your group engage with the material, and more importantly, with one another. Honestly, those kinds of parts are the ones I tend to skip while reading, but I hope you will not.

Each chapter is far from exhaustive, so I have included an extensive bibliography to point you to further resources on each topic. You can also find fuller context for included quotes by referencing the footnotes. Each chapter is brief, pithy, and to the point for another reason; often we only have a moment to interact with unbelievers. In my experience, frequently when I am sharing the Gospel with an unbeliever, I must be brief. I think many of them have already decided they are not very interested in alternative opinions, no matter how discerning or well-reasoned because they reject the overarching claims of Christianity and religions in general.

I have limited myself to thirteen chapters, but atheists believe many silly things. The atheists in your life likely believe one or more of the statements in this volume and some things that are not touched on here. There will probably be a second and even a third volume. But, in the meantime, the Bibliography should be a lot of help for further research, especially for the topics I have not covered.

My position is clear. All the available evidence is plainly on the side of the reality and rulership of the God of the Bible, hence the title of this curriculum. But there are winning and winsome ways of making the truth known, and there are ways of disagreeing that are, quite frankly, repugnant, and offensive; not respecting those who disagree, not serving you well, and harmful (overall) to the cause of Christ.

My intention, throughout this series, is to provide you with more than just a way to win an argument. I want to help you win the heart of a friend or relative who does not know Christ. If you win an argument but verbally annihilate a friend or loved one, you are going about it the wrong way.

Adherence to sound reasoning and critical thinking is a worthwhile goal, but not nearly as important as helping someone embrace a person, the Lord Jesus, who loves them and gave Himself for them. Almost all the chapters include evangelism advice, suggesting ways the myths and slogans many atheists believe may be lovingly corrected, to point them toward the true gospel of the Lord Jesus.

There are a lot of people, on both sides of this issue, that do not think critically, and rationally. That is largely a matter of personal choice. But for Christians, those of us who follow Christ, it's a disobedient choice, because Scripture teaches us to "be ready to give an answer" (1 Peter 3:15) and to study to be approved as workmen who need not be ashamed. (2 Timothy 2:15).

Hopefully, you take those admonitions seriously and this study is only one of many upon which you sharpen your skills for the furtherance of His kingdom. If you love the Savior, feel compassion for fellow image-bearers of God, and take the "Great Commission" seriously, studies like this should be an ongoing part of your ministry preparation. Learning how to witness to all kinds of people, holding various worldviews, is not optional for Christ-followers. It is what we do in response to His call.

Finally, the best way to digest this material is with a group of fellow disciples, for 13 weeks, as your small group curriculum. If you do it that way, please avoid the temptation to read ahead. Follow along at the pace of the group—one chapter per week, occasional supplemental videos, and weekly small group discussions—iron sharpening iron. If you are the group leader, use as many of the questions as are appropriate and possible with your group, and try to do 30% (or less) of the talking during book discussion time.

The 70/30 rule is uncomfortable at first, especially for group members and leaders who are used to learning in a lecture format, but the more closely you follow it, the more likely your group members will benefit from the combined overall wisdom of the group. They are likely to grow far more from the interaction with everyone than from the insight of one, no matter how wise a leader you are.

Be sure to lead the group. Just because you are doing 30%, or less, of the talking does not mean you should be hands off. As a group leader, you should constructively and positively steer the group so that everyone has time to express their opinions and contribute to the lesson. Watch out that no one else jumps in to fill the void and monopolize the conversation. You want the input of every willing member. You also need to ensure the entire time set aside for teaching does not extend past one hour. That is no easy task.

Trust that God speaks to everyone, just like He speaks to you. You will be amazed at the collective insight in the room, even if your group is small. But you must release that insight by providing and creating an atmosphere that invites and encourages contributions from everyone, not just one, all-wise, all-knowing leader.

Small groups are about doing life together as much, or more as consuming and digesting content. Next semester, your group will choose (or be assigned) new content. Your goal is to make the time memorable, socially enriching, intimate, and instructive. If your church has specific emphases, methods, and goals for your group, those supersede these instructions. Your church leaders are trying to produce uniformly enriching groups so that any group someone needs/desires to attend will be a wonderful choice.

Unless you are a subject matter expert, please don't feel the need to position yourself as though you are. The small group is a great place for all members to practice thinking through the material presented. When you model, as the leader, that you are also grappling with, challenged by, and sometimes in disagreement with the material, you give your group members permission to engage at a deeper level.

One word of caution: Don't allow minor disagreements to fester into negativity, either about the content of the class or between members of the group. Nothing destroys a small group, or any size fellowship, quicker than disunity. You are in the group, or leading it, because of the sovereign will of God. Stay positive and uplifting— ready to learn, be challenged, sharpened, and equipped. If you already know everything taught in this material, you are still in the group to grow relationally with other members, to fellowship, pray, and spend time with other believers.

When you disagree with something I have written, preface your remarks with something positive; "I really like this book, and I am so glad we're studying it together. Maybe it's just me, but I had a big problem with X, Y, or Z. Can somebody help me?" You will usually uncover some mixed reactions, some of which you agree with, and others that you don't. My reaction to the way anyone witnesses is sort of like a quote I've seen attributed to Charles Haddon Spurgeon, the gist of it is as follows; "I prefer the way almost anyone shares Christ, to the way most Christians don't."

Chapter One

I Would Believe if There Was Evidence

Before I dive into this first belief, I must make a style announcement. In this curriculum, I write about what atheists say and do not say, and what they believe in both generic and general terms. But when I do, I am not speaking for all atheists. What I write, in each chapter, is not necessarily true for every atheist you encounter. So, whether I make caveats such as, "most," or "many," or for the sake of brevity just say "atheists," or "skeptics," please keep in mind that you will find atheists of varying positions on all the issues raised.

As a committed Christian, I have been witnessing to and talking with self-professed atheists for quite a while. I have Christian friends, enjoy strong Christian fellowship, and I have a decidedly Christian worldview. Living with my feet firmly planted in both worlds, I've noticed a disconnect between the way many of my brothers and sisters view atheists (and atheism), and the way atheists view themselves. Most skeptics believe they are skeptical for scholarly reasons, i.e., a lack of any good evidential reason(s) to believe in God. Many Christians don't buy it. Christians often think atheists are actively suppressing truth, but they (atheists) know better. Atheists, of course, deny the charge. So, who's right? Often, they both are.

Writing to the church at Rome, the Apostle Paul warned, "For the wrath of God is revealed from heaven against all ungodliness and unrighteousness of people who suppress the truth in unrighteousness, because that which is known about God is evident within them; for God made it evident to them." (Romans 1:18, 19). So, honestly, somewhere deep inside their psyches your friendly neighborhood atheist may be suppressing the truth – many are, but what difference does that make?

The Scriptures do not necessarily teach that suppression, due to unrighteousness, is the default position of every atheist. Paul merely states that all of those who were suppressing the truth in unrighteousness are subject to the wrath of God for doing it. But nowhere does Paul indicate to what percentage of atheists the warning applies. But even if it is 100%, atheists who are suppressing truth are almost certainly unaware they're doing it. Their suppression is undoubtedly happening at a subconscious level. If they knew they were suppressing, they wouldn't be atheists. They would be like a lot of backslidden Christians—people who know there is a God and do their best to always avoid Him.

So, while it could technically be true that some atheists are suppressing the truth, and are (therefore) not *really* atheists, for all practical purposes we should treat them like they are. We should extend to them a courtesy they may not return to us, the courtesy of accepting their self-affirmed positions. Those positions comprise a great starting point for probing and constructive discussions. The denial of those positions, especially early on, sets up unnecessary friction that is not conducive to an effective witnessing relationship, or real friendship.

I've heard many Christians tell self-described atheists, "I don't believe you. I know, at some level, you know better." Perhaps you feel that way too. You're sure that somewhere down deep they're faking it. You could even be right. But I've never seen that approach bear fruit. It is insulting, and anything but respectful. The Apostle Peter gave us unambiguous instructions about how to share our faith with those who do not share it. "but sanctify Christ as Lord in your hearts, always being ready to make a defense to everyone who asks you to give an account for the hope that is in you, but with gentleness and respect;" (1 Peter 3:15).

So, assume, as your default position, when an atheist tells you, "I would believe if there was evidence," they are telling you the truth. If you can provide evidence that satisfies them, they are open to receiving the Lord. And yet, I've included this phrase in a book about "silly things atheists believe." If it's true, why is it silly?

"Silly" is wholly subjective. It's in the eye of the beholder. Evidence for God is abundant, so much so that to miss it one must almost be trying. Our atheist friends are deluding themselves with the notion that their only objection is a lack of (what they consider) evidence. I cover a similar, connected objection in more detail in chapter two, and what constitutes "evidence" is discussed there. Although it's usually not productive to talk with them about it, many atheists admit that if God appeared in the sky in front of them, transported them immediately to His level, told them something private that only He could know, then told them to receive the Lord Jesus, they would still not believe. They would find some alternative explanation to explain what just happened because practically anything is preferable to believing in God. But why?

First, just like every Christian, every atheist is a huge sinner – COLOSSAL – not just the small stuff. Sin ruins everything it touches, and the sin that, in many ways, is at the root of all others is PRIDE. I have never met an atheist who is not riddled with pride, and I've met a bunch of them. They are proud of their exceptional knowledge. They are proud of their intelligence. Sometimes they are proud of their "go against the grain," counter-cultural stance, as an atheist. They are proud of their lifestyle choices – proud of their associations, and proud of their imagined superiority, especially over believers. Sometimes they have enough self-awareness to recognize how unattractive pride is, so they mask it in various ways, but often it's one of the first things you'll notice. This regrettable pride, by the way, is not materially different from that held by a great number of Christians. It's an unfortunate byproduct of the human condition. I don't even point it out as a put-down, but to help you see through the delusion.

Pride is the root, but further sin, of various kinds is usually the fruit. In verse 28 of the first chapter of Romans, Paul wrote, "And just as they did not see fit to acknowledge God, God gave them up to a depraved mind, to do those things that are not proper." I have discovered, especially when someone embraces atheism after appearing to be a Christian, that they have usually come to a decision (at some level) that acknowledging God will only serve to remind them of their sinfulness, an anxious state their pride refuses to endure. So, in their quest to flee God's authority, they are willing to grasp at and endorse every complaint, false notion, argument, and slogan against Him. I'm also convinced it is pride that will not allow our atheist friends to admit, even to themselves, what's really going on. I've done numerous exit interviews and read many more, and this cognitive disconnect is almost always recognized, but only after a person surrenders to Christ.

So, while they often don't recognize it, it is not a lack of evidence keeping most atheists away. In fact, in this era when knowledge is exploding, there are more and more empirical reasons to believe in God. One would have to be actively dismissing and discounting these reasons, intentionally avoiding interacting with them, turning a blind eye and a deaf ear toward them, and that's (frequently) exactly what's happening.

There's an additional phrase that goes with this one: "Believe me, I wish there was a God. I would *love* for it to be true, but there's *no* evidence that it is." Words to that effect are the mainstay of many atheists. And commonly they're trying to convince themselves, each time they repeat them, that they are sincere followers of truth, awaiting more evidence, all the while actively rejecting the abundant evidence that is already available. And, while we may feel we have some understanding of the underlying psychology, it's important to approach every skeptic on their own terms, accepting their self-described thoughts and inclinations—to win a person, not an argument.

The reason I have armed you with some insights into the mind of an atheist is not so you will accuse them of lying (even to themselves), but so that you'll understand that they are not such a peculiar category that in reaching them the gospel has somehow lost its power or is not enough. Whatever else has become a smokescreen for them, the barrier between them and God is the same one that yours was – sin. The less time you spend on the smokescreens and subterfuge, and the sooner you get to the remedy, the better off they may be. You need to be ready to talk about their objections, but not obsessed with those complaints to the exclusion of the gospel. The goal of every encounter, as often as possible, whenever possible, is to make a beeline to the cross.

A Winning Approach

Our conjectures and anecdotal knowledge of the atheist's state of mind are, at times, a helpful backdrop to remind us to keep the main thing the main thing – to aim conversationally toward the universal need for forgiveness and to dig deeper than surface objections. In Acts 17, we find a model case study of how that's done. The Apostle Paul was witnessing in a pluralistic religious environment. Although the polytheists he was addressing were not atheists, they were just as deeply entrenched in their worldview(s).

If you've read much about Paul and considered his approach, you know the cross is central to it. Ten quick verses (22-31) summarize his message to a wide variety of idol worshippers at the Areopagus in Athens, Greece. That message is winsome, urgent, relatable, and bold – finding and capitalizing on common ground, explaining the nature of

God, the problem of our estrangement from Him, and the remedy of the cross. It's a wonderful case study of how to share Christ powerfully and effectively.

Our tendency, when reading such messages, is to put Paul in a special category that both excludes and excuses us. "I wish I could think of the right things to say, and always had just the right words, but I'm not Paul." "I wasn't given the 'gift of gab,'" or "I don't think well 'on my feet.'" Paul was heroic. Me? Not so much.

I am bothered by the truth that Paul may have just cared more than I do. What if he prepared more than I do? Paul knew there was a pluralistic meeting of the minds at the Areopagus in Athens. This seedbed of philosophical and religious cross-pollination was known throughout the region. As someone who teaches and speaks for a living, I assume Paul spent some time considering how best to arrest and keep the attention of the people with whom he would be speaking. I imagine he prayed about how to reach them. He probably spoke to believers who had interacted with people in that environment. He may have even asked around, and dipped his toes into the cultural milieu, because he quoted popular poets – kind of the modern equivalent of relating his thesis to current song lyrics. Paul followed his own advice to be diligent and present himself approved to God, as an unashamed servant (2 Timothy 2:15). He did his homework and honed his skills.

> So Paul stood in the midst of the Areopagus and
> said, "Men of Athens, I see that you are very
> religious in all respects. 23 For while I was
> passing through and examining the objects of
> your worship, I also found an altar with this

inscription, 'TO AN UNKNOWN GOD.' Therefore, what you worship in ignorance, this I proclaim to you. 24 The God who made the world and everything that is in it, since He is Lord of heaven and earth, does not dwell in temples made by hands; 25 nor is He served by human hands, as though He needed anything, since He Himself gives to all people life and breath and all things; 26 and He made from one man every nation of mankind to live on all the face of the earth, having determined their appointed times and the boundaries of their habitation, 27 that they would seek God, if perhaps they might feel around for Him and find Him, though He is not far from each one of us; 28 for in Him we live and move and exist, as even some of your own poets have said, 'For we also are His descendants.' 29 Therefore, since we are the descendants of God, we ought not to think that the Divine Nature is like gold or silver or stone, an image formed by human skill and thought. 30 So having overlooked the times of ignorance, God is now proclaiming to mankind that all people everywhere are to repent, 31 because He has set a day on which He will judge the world in righteousness through a Man whom He has appointed, having furnished proof to all people by raising Him from the dead." (Acts 17:22-31).

If Paul's sermon introduction (vss. 22-23) sounds a bit harsh, like he's launching with an intolerant opening salvo, perhaps some context would help it make more sense. Paul was speaking at the equivalent of a modern "free speech" forum. His opening statement was supposed to stake out a debating position that further interaction would test and defend. Since he was speaking to everyone who would listen, he was also speaking to no one in particular. In that sense he was non-confrontational. Comparing his presentation to others he made, and to presentations from Christ and others of the Apostles, we can learn an important strategy, one espoused by Paul, to "become all things to all people, so that I may by all means save some." (1 Corinthians 19:22b), in other words, to tailor your approach to your environment.

I think Paul was winsome. He almost had to be, as he was calling for people to abandon their gods and realign their entire worldview. But winsome is not always a synonym for self-effacing, verbal egg-shell walking. Sometimes the environment demands a confident statement of what you know to be so. You should be *inoffensive*, or at least not *intentionally* offensive, but to some people, any correction or factual disagreement is offensive, whether intended to be or not.[2]

It's an uncomfortable fact of witnessing that you know something someone else doesn't, and what you know is critically important to their well-being. You, therefore, do them little good when you pretend you only know it tentatively, even if you're trying to be inoffensive and approachable. Striking the right tone between "possessor of important truth" and "open to new information" is difficult, but it gets easier the more you witness.

In verses 24 and 25 Paul begins his case for God with general logic about what *kind* of God He must *necessarily* be. He challenges the

---

[2] Taking offense is common and left unchecked can be a conversation defeater. Here is a phrase I've often found helpful. "I didn't mean to offend you and I sincerely apologize, but I do love talking with you. I hope we can get past it. Help me with my understanding: Why is it okay for you to disagree strongly with me, but offensive for me to disagree strongly with you?"

logic that anyone worthy of the title (God) could live in something carved or otherwise fashioned by one of His creatures. In Christian Apologetics terms, Paul is making the logical general case for God – in this case, a specific kind of God since his audience was already comprised of god (little g) believers.

But Paul's task was not merely to posit that *a* god exists. In verse 26 He told his audience that the God of Whom He spoke was not an exalted creation, like the Greek and Roman gods and goddesses, but rather THE Creator of all mankind – the Instigator. The God Whom Paul represents *is* the "Ground of all being," the Singular, Sole, non-contingent Being – the One Who made, upholds, and rules over all. Today, we might use philosophical arguments, such as the "argument from contingency," historical arguments (about the life of Christ and testimony of the early church), and scientific arguments such as implications and inferences drawn from cosmology and DNA, to make the same points.

Perhaps Paul was "sizing up" his audience. He may have noticed a few of them starting to nod off. Or, he may have already decided that he was going to work some popular poetry into his speech. Either way, that's what he does in verses 27-28. First, he alludes to Epimenides the Cretan, a poet whom he also cited in Titus 1:12. Epimenides' original poem is no longer extant, but we know about it because quite a few ancient writers also quoted from it. Next, he cited Aratus, another Greek poet of Soli in Cilicia. Writing about a pantheistic god, Aratus' line, "in him we move and live and have our being," was appropriated by Paul to make a statement about Jehovah

God as the source of all life. The witnessing application is obvious: he found common ground and friendly affinity with his audience. What Paul was saying was too important to waste on an audience that wasn't listening. It was also so important that Paul wasn't "shooting from the hip," unrehearsed and/or unprepared. He didn't come to play.

In the remainder of his sermon, Paul reiterated his logic challenging the worth of false idols (vs. 29), indicated the need for personal repentance (vs. 30), warned of future accountability (judgment) and preached the identity of the Lord Jesus as proven by His resurrection (vs. 31). All of that represented a radical departure from the current worldviews of his audience, yet history shows, and the Scriptures record that while there were some scoffers on that day, there were also those who "joined him and believed, among whom also were Dionysius the Areopagite and a woman named Damaris, and others with them." (Acts 17:34b). The conversion of Dionysius led, no doubt, to many more, as he (Dionysius) became the first Bishop of Athens, and to this day there are large churches in Athens that bear his name.

The *secret* to seeing skeptics embrace faith in Christ is not all that complicated: No matter what the stated objection(s), regardless of how stringently someone protests, if they are willing to have a civil conversation, you should proceed. Be gentle, and kind, but unwavering, assume they're honest, and address their objections. Share Christ under the control of the Spirit, unafraid to employ the power of Scripture, and keep making a beeline for the cross. In many ways, atheists are not materially different from other people who *believe* in God but *refuse* to receive Him. When you engage them in civil discourse some will scoff, some will wait for a more opportune time, and some, bless the Lord, will believe, repent, and receive.

IMPORTANT: When your friend, relative, associate, or neighbor says, "I would believe if there was evidence," they have thrown down a gauntlet from which you must not recoil. The most logical question, when you've heard such a statement, is "What kinds of evidence for God have you studied?" In my experience, most of the time, they haven't studied evidence at all because they've fallen for another silly thing atheists believe, the erroneous notion that "there's no evidence for God." Read on brave one.

I Would Believe if There Was Evidence

1. Ask everyone in the group to give a quick report on how they're doing this week, spiritually, emotionally, and physically.

2. Let's test the idea that personal sin sometimes leads to a personal denial of God. Poll your group with this question. Have you ever had a faith crisis, where you were in some danger of forsaking belief in God? Looking back, what do you think contributed to that?

3. What's your story? Has pride ever reared its ugly head and caused problems in your life? Can you think of a specific time and/or place? What happened?

4. What are some reasons, even though we accept skeptics at their word, that it's helpful to think through what may be subconsciously behind their decisions?

5. What could you do in the next seven days to help prepare the ground for your witness to someone who is off in sin, running from Christ?

6. Do you have any favorite parts of this chapter you would like to discuss further?

Pray for the mental, spiritual, and physical needs of those in your sphere of influence. Ask God to give you genuine, caring friendships based on mutual love and respect, with people who are far from Him.

Chapter Two

There's No Evidence for God

Careful readers may see a developing pattern. Our atheist friends are mentally/emotionally safe while asserting, pending convincing evidence, a willingness to acquiesce to God. Quite simply, they are all but certain such evidence, just like God Himself, is non-existent. So, for them, the whole point is moot. God is no more real than the tooth fairy – sorry kids.

To my knowledge, while I was growing up (ages 6-17) in a small midwestern city, I knew only one atheist. He was the dad of one of my friends at school, whom I will call "Jim," not his actual name. I now know that Jim, who is a strong Christian today, was also an atheist back then. Most kids pretty much embrace whatever their parents believe, at least until they are old enough to start forming opinions of their own.

I do remember assuming at that time that Jim himself knew better than his dad and must have been embarrassed about his dad's odd deviation from what (to us) was the obvious truth that there is a God. Few of us spoke to Jim about either his dad or God, because Jim was a wonderfully likable and good friend to everyone in our class. We did not want to single him out because of his dad's odd behavior.

Even though the Supreme Court had disallowed faculty-led prayer in schools in 1963, from 1964 until at least the early seventies we were still led, each morning in the "Lord's Prayer" in our classrooms, and I do not recall ever once considering whether Jim might have been uncomfortable with that.

Jim's dad was a professor at the local university and highly intelligent. Even on the university campus in those days (the sixties and seventies) he was pretty much in a class all his own. My dad, who was also a professor, spoke of him as "stubborn." That's probably not the word he used. Knowing my dad, I am sure he never spoke of him pejoratively, but I still got the impression that Jim's dad held ridiculous views, so far out of the mainstream, that no one even needed to bother rebutting them. It was as if everyone knew that he had to know better but he was just being stubborn.

So, in my young mind, there was a huge disconnect. How could this man be so smart and so seemingly stupid at the same time? Of course, now I know he was anything but stupid. But remember, at the time, I was – relative to this discussion and material – an ignorant child.

Jim's dad was heavily influenced by a strain of philosophical thought that at its core believes in an intrinsic fallacy: There is no evidence that God exists. That statement is practically an atheist mantra. Most of them think it is true, although many people who think so have never given it much serious thought. They have rarely honestly considered the numerous volumes by scholars writing on the opposite side of the one they are taking. That is often the nature of a mantra or a slogan. It becomes reflexive and is regularly assumed to be true despite a lack of empirical support.

Statements repeated over and over frequently have the consequence, whether intended or not, of appearing true. Beginning sometime in the late 1950's some advertising genius decided that Coca Cola™ was "the pause that refreshes," and due to heavy advertising to that effect millions of people, around the world prefer a cold Coke™ to a glass of water even though the former depletes us and arguably makes us thirstier. Once a slogan-like ball gets rolling it becomes very difficult to derail or to stop its forward momentum.

As for the notion that there is no evidence for God, one of the main philosophers credited with getting that ball rolling is David Hume, an 18th-century Scottish philosopher. Long before Frederic Nietzsche, and others were proclaiming "God is dead," Hume was deconstructing the basics of Christianity, asserting that every foundation upon which it was built was either entirely false or severely flawed.

As an empiricist, Hume saw no good reason to believe any human knowledge came by way of revelation but instead, he proffered it was wholly the result of human experience. He also opposed the teleological argument (the argument from design) for God's existence with a ferocity that had not been previously seen. Moreover, he argued that even the world's great monotheistic religions, Judaism, Christianity, and Islam, were derived from earlier polytheistic religions and that they largely represented man's reaction to the fear of the unknown, not an external revelation of God. Of course, Hume's most well-known argument, and the reason even non-philosophers have heard of him, is his argument against the possibility of miracles.

While none of that disproves God, if Hume was right, God had not revealed Himself, had not designed and created the universe, offered nothing truly new - religiously speaking - and did nothing miraculous. For all intents and purposes that might as well be a non-existent god. In any event, he's certainly not the God of the Bible. It took more than a few years to get to the "no evidence for God" slogan but the precursors were present in the work of Hume.

Ironically, in the nearly 250 years since his death, there have been no "silver bullet" or "paradigm-busting" discoveries from science, history, or philosophy to suggest he was on to something. Nevertheless, once an idea gets rolling it becomes nearly impossible to derail. So, atheists have been asserting, with no good evidence, for at least 100 years now that there is no good evidence for God.

In my experience when you present the evidence, they have one of two responses: 1. They assert, with no substantive rebuttal, "That is not evidence." Or, 2. They say something to the effect of, "Don't give me that garbage. That's been debunked for years," which they almost always say, again, without offering a clue as to the content of the alleged rebuttal.

I will introduce you to some of the actual evidence for God in subsequent chapters of this manual, but for now, the reason it is a silly thing to believe is that it is just a slogan, not an argument. All the various arguments posited for God's existence are within the definition of evidence. One can argue that they fail in some way, but one should not nonsensically assert that they are not evidence.

One could even say, "I have considered the evidence, and I am not persuaded by it," but it is silly to say, "There is no evidence for God," which is why that saying – quite prevalent among atheists – is included in this book.

We must understand why they say such a silly thing. Atheists cannot mentally or emotionally allow a supernatural foot in the door. On a psychological level, they must use superlatives and grandiose unproven, and unprovable statements because they want to slam the door shut and stop thinking about the things that should be keeping them up restless most nights.

I have a simple question I use to try to help skeptics face their insecurities and reconsider the "evidence" slogan: "Are you referring to the dictionary definition of the word 'evidence' or some non-standard personal definition?" When I use this question online, I am largely ignored, but when I ask it face-to-face there is almost always an adjustment and an acknowledgment to something such as, "Well, there is not anything I think is very persuasive." Fine, but that is not nearly the same and now we are getting somewhere.

Greg Koukl, the author of Tactics, says that his goal in witnessing encounters is to "put a stone in the shoe" of the person to whom he is witnessing.[3] He is not trying to win them. That is above our pay grade anyway. That is a great and worthy goal. People do not usually become skeptical in one encounter with irrational and unreasonable concepts, books, and materials. It usually takes a lot of indoctrination to reject

---

[3] Gregory Koukl, *Tactics: A Game Plan for Discussing Your Christian Convictions* (Grand Rapids, MI: Zondervan, 2009), 38.

something as plain as the fact that there must be a God.

It takes a sort of intellectual disconnect for most people to look into the night sky, or at flowers, birds, trees, and newborn babies and conclude that all of this is a cosmic accident without a Beginner or a beginning. Having that degree of dissonance between their thinking and reasonable/rational thought it is probably an immodest goal to get them "all straightened out," so to speak, if you can just "get them to listen." A much better approach is to help your skeptical friend or relative see a little more clearly, think a little more reasonably, and just maybe, in the case of this silly thing they may be believing, to understand that it is a slogan but not an argument.

Although I keep up with Jim and one of his sisters through Facebook, I have never asked them what became of their dad. To be honest, I fear it could be a sore spot that may be uncomfortable for them to talk about. But I do know that Jim's sister grew up to work for a Christian ministry—to love, serve, and worship the Lord Jesus and so did Jim. If there was any actual evidence for atheism you would think these people were exposed to it, year after year, during all their formative days.

Instead, they saw that it was an intellectually deficient and bankrupt system. Atheists say, "We make no positive claims and therefore have no burden of proof," but then turn around and positively claim, "There is no evidence for God." To make that claim stick they need meaningful, substantive rebuttals for the many sound and reasonable arguments for God. They do not have them, and such a statement is a silly slogan, not a meaningful argument.

One problem for atheism is the "argument from contingency." Simply put, we know of nothing that exists that is not contingent. Everything came from something else. Acorns grow trees, which in turn produce acorns. Every oak tree started with an acorn – without exception, except there must have been an original oak tree before the first acorn, or vice versa.

Consider the panoply of nature, whether evolving or staying the same, as the passing boxcars in a train – each boxcar connected (causally) to the previous one. We know the number of boxcars cannot be infinite. If we go back far enough, there is an engine that started the whole thing rolling. Logically, the same must be said of nature itself. If there is nothing beyond, or in addition to nature then nature "started" itself. Yet one implication of the cosmological Big Bang is that nature did have a beginning, an inference that is quite troubling to the core of atheism, as most atheists assert that nature is all there is.

The opening sentence in the late Carl Sagan's best-selling book, Cosmos, is "The Cosmos is all that is or ever was or ever will be."[4] As it turns out, according to the argument from contingency, and inferences drawn from the big bang, that was perhaps an inaccurate statement. That's how atheists would like the world to be, but that statement does not seem to match with what science is demonstrating. English astronomer, physicist, and mathematician, the late Sir Arthur Stanley Eddington clearly identified the problems (for atheism) associated with this one observation. "Philosophically, the notion of a

---

[4] Carl Sagan, *Cosmos* (New York, NY: Ballantine, 1980), 1.

beginning of the present order of Nature is repugnant to me . . . I should like to find a genuine loophole."[5]

Eddington saw if we are ever going to find a starting place for nature itself it would have to be something that exists (or existed) outside of nature, and he saw the problem that presents to atheism since empirical observation indicates every reaction was caused by an action – every beginning needs a Beginner, or at the very least a plausible explanation. Nobel Laureate (Physics) Arno Penzias, when interviewed by *the New York Times* famously stated, "The best data we have are exactly what I would have predicted had I nothing to go on but the five books of Moses, the Psalms, and the Bible as a whole."[6]

"Evidence" corroborated by history, experience, science, philosophy, testimony, logic, and reason is more than sufficient for court, and even sufficient for most atheists when supporting a point about which they agree. It's either not enough or dismissed entirely, however, when pointing to the high likelihood that there is a God Who exists, Who reveals Himself through the Hebrew and Christian Scriptures, by His Holy Spirit, and through past and present interactions with His creation.

Of course, in whatever way everything began, the position of naturalists is that matter gave rise to mind. Matter developed, through the evolutionary process, into greater and more complex systems,

---

[5] Arthur S. Eddington, "The End of the World from the Standpoint of Mathematical Physics," *Nature* 127 (1931): 450.
[6] Malcolm W. Browne, "Clues to Universe Origin Expected; The Making of the Universe," *New York Times*, March 12, 1978.

currently culminating in evolution's most self-aware development – humankind. While scientists have not yet solved abiogenesis, the problem of how it all started, atheists are confident it can be (solved), without resorting to any hypothesis exceeding nature itself.

Dr. John Lennox, a Christian statesman, Oxford professor of mathematics, and philosopher of science sees the issue as follows:

> . . . my claim is that it is the exact opposite way around. Mind is primary in the universe. God is the ultimate reality. Everything else, including you and me is derivative, so that means that here's the claim, let me set it out. In the beginning was the Word, the Word was with God, the Word was God. All things were made by Him.[7]

Dr. Lennox is looking at the same science, but he is viewing it without the psychologically pressing need to find a "loophole," since he is also personally aware that the God many atheists are desperately avoiding does exist. To conclude "there's no evidence for God," one must either redefine the word "evidence," or substantively rebut reams of evidence, from various fields and disciplines which cumulatively infer His existence. Some of the better-educated, more scholarly atheists admit that the inferences about God are strong, even if their preferences and inclinations prefer to posit more attractive alternative explanations.

To simply parrot the slogan, "there is no evidence," is not only false, . . . an overstatement, but unscholarly and ill-informed. Many sound arguments inductively infer His existence. Such arguments are

---

[7] *Dawkins vs. Lennox: The God Delusion Debate*

the same kinds of arguments prosecuting attorneys offer to support their theory of a case based on the totality of what is known about it, drawing an inference, considering known facts, to the best explanation.

That is also the way atheists decide other (more mundane) day-to-day matters. Yet, for assorted reasons, having more to do with passions and psychology than with reason, logic, or intelligence, atheists seem (mostly) unwilling to apply the same methods to their process when considering the God question. Like Sir Eddington, they prefer the "loophole" to the obvious implications and inferences drawn from the preponderance of empirical data.

In other words, atheists are like many Christians. In several ways, they are just like you and me. They are flawed, finite people. Like me, their pride looks for ways to have their way, call their shots, and be their bosses. Christians may protest, "I have been radically changed by Christ," and He does conform us to Himself, but that is a long and (usually) slow process. The surest way to see how servant-hearted you are is to monitor how you feel/respond when someone treats you like a servant. Even if you are in a better place now, your BC (before Christ) life was markedly corrupted by your inappropriate (even) evil desires, and your lust for personal validation no matter how wrong you were.

All atheists are similarly stained people who are trying to justify themselves, trying (in their pride) for an alternate solution to the human condition. Just like you, the maintenance of their worldview and their personal psychology depends on them convincing themselves of the truths of their propositions. No atheist is your adversary, even those who think they are. They are fellow citizens of earth, image-bearers of

God, in need of His mercy, for whom Christ died.

They have a lot riding on the truth of their slogan, "There's no evidence for God," for if it is not true their worldview and concepts of self are at grave risk. You must not cavalierly dismiss it, or worse, pejoratively characterize those who claim they believe it. One cannot simply destroy or devastate a worldview without causing harm to those holding it.

We should present our case for Christ and Christianity in some totality, with an assurance that it can bear the weight of the hopes, expectations, and base needs of those who are considering it as a replacement for the one they (currently) hold. Your mileage may vary, but my experience with atheists has shown me that it takes several encounters with truth, . . . wrestling, struggling, debating, and reasoning through the Scriptures, logic, and evidence, because the worldview they are embracing was constructed, over an extended period, against their intuition, opposed to their innate knowledge, and the witness of His (God's) Spirit and yes, despite strong evidence to the contrary.

Like "the pause that refreshes" the slogan, "there's no evidence for God" has stuck for a variety of reasons, but the strongest one is that it fits a desire for how someone wants the world to be. I would like to believe, for example, that drinking liquid candy, full of corn sweetener, will replenish and refresh my dehydrated body more than God's elixir, good ol' H_2O. It will not, but I am going to need time for that to sink in because I love an ice-cold soft drink and my gut bacteria crave sugar. Even when I become (sort of) convinced I must be wrong, I am stuck in old, comfortable patterns that keep me guzzling soda several times a day. It is even harder to get unstuck from a worldview endorsed by your echo chamber of friends and elitists, and in which Satan—your very real enemy, wants to keep you ensnared.

Reason alone might not break the spell. Your atheist friend does not realize it, but they need prayer warriors, fasting and praying for their deliverance, for the eyes of their understanding to be opened, for multiple harvest laborers to cross the path of their life, and for God to arrest not only their attention but their heart to the fearful, sinful condition they are in. And they need you, dear reader, both to "study to show yourself approved" and to "pray to the Lord" of that harvest. They need you to be aware that life is a battlefield (not a playground), and to pray and work accordingly.

There is no Evidence for God

1. Which Bible or movie character are you feeling most like today, and why?

2. Why might it be psychologically important for a skeptic to believe there is no evidence for God?

3. Are Christians sometimes also guilty of uncritically accepting unproven slogans? How? What should churches be doing to help Christians think through issues, problems, and barriers to faith?

4. What should our approach and demeanor be when confronting this mindset, especially because we are also guilty of falling for slogans that influence our thoughts and reasoning?

5. What, if anything, should the author have done differently when his childhood friend's family were likely all atheists? Would the confrontation, questioning, and reasoning of a relatively uninformed child have mattered much, one way or another? What responsibility do more mature Christians have toward their unbelieving friends and family?

Pray for the person God has put on your heart or is leading you to. Ask the Lord to make them receptive to a deeper, more substantive, and open relationship with you and with Him.

Chapter Three

Faith is a Synonym for Gullibility

Faith may be one of the least understood words in Christendom. We refer to our belief system and worldview as the "Christian faith." Jesus indicated that it only took a small amount of this substance or quality to move mountains or attack stubborn problems and situations. He commended people for "much" faith, and He chided them for "little" faith. The writer of Hebrews defined faith as "assurance" and "evidence" (11:1). It is the root of "faithfulness," which is an admirable quality, and perhaps the most important attribute of a healthy marriage. But for all of that, it may surprise you to know that many atheists, when they congratulate you for having more faith than they have, are not genuinely impressed. Many of them think your faith is a weakness, not a strength. That's often because they define faith wholly differently than you do.

We should not fault our atheist friends for redefining/mis-defining faith. Their definition is not unlike at least one of the entries (for faith) in a good dictionary. Besides that, due in no small way to the growth of the "Word of Faith" movement, quite a few Christians are also confused about what faith is. Like most words, there are multiple definitions. But the definition the average atheist thinks Christians are employing is feasibly not the definition one could logically derive from Scripture. Faith is not a synonym for gullibility. It is not the act of believing things that are patently absurd, or of believing despite a lack of good evidence.

Some writers have gone as far as to attribute our ability to have faith to a "faith gene," or "God gene." To atheists, people who have that gene may simply not be able to help it, but they are poor, pitiful, deluded fools—helplessly believing utter nonsense. Given enough time, human evolution will breed out the faith gene and all of humanity will step out of the dark ages of superstitious, unfounded beliefs into the light of reason. While it is beyond the scope of this volume to examine those arguments in detail, prepared witnesses must be aware of them. If you speak to skeptics often, they will eventually tell you that you only believe because you are genetically hardwired for belief, and they cannot believe because they are not. They simply lack the "faith gene."

So far, the "God gene" hypothesis is supported by only one, quite controversial study, conducted by geneticist Dean Hamer, the results and methodology of which is published in his book, *The God Gene: How Faith is Hardwired Into Our Genes.*[8] Hamer's conclusions are even dismissed by the famous atheist biologist PZ Myers, who wrote about the specific gene Hamer identifies, "Yes,

---

[8] Dean Hamer, *The God Gene: How Faith Is Hardwired into Our Genes* (New York, NY: Anchor Books, 2005)

it's important, and it may even be active and necessary during higher order processing, like religious thought. But one thing it isn't is a 'god gene.'"[9] Science writer, Carl Zimmer has also criticized the theory as being "based on only one unpublished, unreplicated study."[10]

Even if proven true a "God gene" could just as easily be construed as additional evidence *for* a God who left a marker for Himself at the level of DNA. The fact that not everyone still carries such a marker, on the Christian worldview, could be chalked up to a result of the fall of mankind. To his credit, even Hamer quite clearly writes, "This book is about whether God genes exist, not about whether there is a God."[11] This controversial gene may, at best, contribute to the acceptance of God, but whether it plays a more important role than nurture, environment, experience, knowledge, or the Holy Spirit is certainly unsettled, even if it's proven such a gene exists.

Sometimes atheists seem to be working against themselves. On the one hand, they like to assert that people are believing because of evolutionary genetic defects, making belief probable even though the evidence does not warrant it. But they are also fond of asserting that the concept of God must be indoctrinated into children and that without such indoctrination it would not occur to them. Much to

---

[9] Myers, PZ (2005-02-13). "No god, and no 'god gene', either". *Pharyngula*. Archived from the original on October 3, 2009.

[10] Zimmer, Carl (October 2004). "Faith-Boosting Genes: A search for the genetic basis of spirituality". *Scientific American*.

[11] Dean Hamer, *The God Gene: How Faith Is Hardwired into Our Genes* (New York, NY: Anchor Books, 2005), 16.

their chagrin, there are several studies suggesting that is not so. Oxford University Psychologist Olivera Petrovich performed one such highly controversial analysis. She performed her study by surveying the literature of numerous international studies of children from four to seven years of age. She determined that belief in a "creator" God is the default setting and that "atheism is an acquired position."[12] Such findings fly in the face of those (atheists) who insist that religious indoctrination is to blame for whatever knowledge of God they cannot explain by the "god gene" hypothesis.

The "god gene" proposition is one reason it may not be a compliment when your atheist friend says, "I just do not have your faith." What they may *mean* is that they are more evolved and enlightened. They have genetically progressed beyond believing in your superstitious nonsense. Your faith, far from being enviable, is pitiable. But their definition of faith is often inaccurate. That is too bad for a couple of reasons:

1) When we use the same words to mean different things, we are not communicating *with* each other. We are talking *past* one another.

That situation reminds me of an old Saturday Night Live skit,[13] during the days of the original cast. Gilda Radner's character, Rosanna Rosanna Danna, was railing, at length in a *Weekend Update* editorial, about how silly it was to be upset or disturbed by "violins" on

---

[12] See Barney Zwartz, "Infants 'Have Natural Belief in God,'" *Sydney Morning Herald*, July 26, 2008, https://www.smh.com.au/national/infnts-have-natural-belief-in-god-20080725-313b.html; also refer to Olivera Petrovich's book, *Natural-Theological Understanding from Childhood to Adulthood: Essays in Developmental Psychology* (London: Routledge, 2019).
[13] A long-running American television sketch comedy program.

television. After all, they add to the drama and the impact of a great love scene, conveying more of the emotions that each character is experiencing. She goes on at length until Chevy Chase realizes what she is saying and corrects her error. "It's not 'violins' we're concerned with. It's VIOLENCE!" "Oh," she docilely replies, "Never mind."

2) The second reason a wrong definition is bad for progress is that it disadvantages our skeptical friends by making them argue a "straw man," or caricature of our position.

A "straw man" argument distorts someone's position and then argues against the distortion rather than against the actual position held. Thinking Christians are not exercising "blind faith," or faith without good evidence. The Biblical definition of faith includes substantive reasons for exercising that faith. A better English word, conveying the Biblical viewpoint for faith, is the word "trust." We only trust, or place faith, in that for which we have good reasons to believe our trust is warranted.

So, when we read in the eleventh chapter of Hebrews that "By faith" certain things happened, a better, or more accurate translation would be "Because they trusted." Because he trusted God Abel brought Him a better sacrifice (vs. 4). Because He trusted God, Enoch was taken from this life, not experiencing death (vs. 5), and so on.

Much of the proof, not only that God exists but of Who God is, we find in the life of the Lord Jesus. The Father did not merely send Jesus to teach us the attributes of God, the commandments, and the Scriptures. He sent the Lord Jesus to display a pattern and a life that offered up proof and evidence that His Words were more than conjecture or opinion. A well-known Christian Apologist, Dr. Frank Turek, often says, "I tend to pay attention when someone who rises from the dead talks to me about God."[14] The life of Jesus is a piece of the evidence God offers to prove that His revelation of Himself is true. His control over nature, sickness, infirmities, disease, and even death are all indicative of His status and stature as a Spokesman without parallel or equal. When speaking about the nature of reality, particularly metaphysics, He demonstrated His authority and knowledge were unsurpassed.

It is no wonder, given the definition of faith that many atheists have— "believing in something without good evidence"—that several of them see that (faith) as a synonym for gullibility. This, they reason, and rightly so, is no substitute for empirically verifiable data, and the "real world" of empiricism, events, matter, history, and science. By their definition, it is not a silly thing atheists believe that people should not believe things – anything – without evidence. We should agree with them when confronted with this accusation, but agree by agreeably disagreeing with their larger premise, that such "faith," more accurately defined as blind faith, is indeed what the Scriptures commend Christians for practicing.

---

[14] An oft-repeated part of Dr. Turek's presentation, "I Don't Have Enough Faith to be an Atheist."

When confronted with this atheist's slogan a helpful response might be to say, "You're certainly right. Such faith is no way to arrive at the truth. I would even say it's entirely backward to try to believe in something you truly know little or nothing about." If you want some "brownie points" you might also admit that many Christians agree with their definition. "I think you're almost certainly right about that. I've met many Christians who seem to be defining faith poorly. But I don't think it's a definition warranted by close examination of the Scriptures. Do you mind if I offer you the definition I use?" Memorize this, word-for-word, "Biblical faith is exercising trust in God, based on good reasons to believe He is trustworthy." It is important, as you offer this definition, that your tone, demeanor, and attitude be one of polite, respectful, even gentle conversation, not argumentative domination, or annihilation.

Even though some Christians are defining faith improperly they may still not be guilty of just (gullibly) *blindly* accepting Jesus. Many Christians originally trust in Christ because of a strong, confirming witness of the Holy Spirit, something that is personal and, from the viewpoint of someone not experiencing it, subjective, but very moving, real, and convincing, at least to those who have experienced it. Once that has happened, Christians are given a further advantage: The Holy Spirit, Whom Jesus referred to as the "Spirit of Truth" comes to live in us, giving us the ability to see an amazing array of evidence that had always been around us, with new clarity and insight. We often start to see evidence in places where atheists' eyes have not yet been opened. As C. S. Lewis wrote, "I believe in

Christianity as I believe that the Sun has risen, not only because I see it but because by it, I see everything else."[15]

I designed a T-shirt that says, "Blind Faith is Not Biblical Faith." But that is only partially true. Saving (or initial) faith is not blind faith, but once someone knows the Lord it is often perfectly appropriate to trust Him wherever He is leading next, even if one does not yet know where that is, how hard the trip will be, or when they may arrive. The details of each step of a journey are unimportant if I am following a trusted and trustworthy Guide.

I often use my marriage as an illustration. I know my wife well enough to know I can trust her heart. Whatever she promises me I can count on her doing it. Moreover, as all analogies break down, I can trust the Lord much more because nothing is too hard for Him. But the point is my trust is built on our relationship. If you're not married, you certainly have a trusted friend or confidant. Trusting someone is a simple matter of vetting them properly, and knowing their history, character, and attributes.

The most common atheist's response is that we do not know anything about God, since He cannot be seen, empirically investigated, or proven. That response is called "begging the question" and it is a logical fallacy. If one says, one reason I know there is a God is that He responds to me, has spoken to me, has healed, or touched me in some way, it is improper to say, "No, it can't be God because you have no evidence He exists." Why? I am offering my

---

[15] C. S. Lewis, *The Weight of Glory* (New York, NY: Harper Collins, 1949), 140.

experiences of Him as (at least) part of the evidence you claim does not exist. The topic being considered is whether there is a God or not. To simply dismiss the argument offered, or automatically assume its failure before considering the merits is unfair. And besides, there are a lot of good reasons to assume God's existence and arguably only a couple to think He may not exist. Those two are too involved to be discussed at length in this volume, but you can read more about them in many of the books listed in the bibliography at the end of this book.

There are also especially good reasons to assume His trustworthiness, not the least of which is the recorded historical testimony of the church throughout over twenty centuries. This eyewitness, personal, experiential testimony is represented in, by far, the most voluminous documentation of any phenomenon in human history. Christ's followers have (repeatedly) been making claims that are so similar and so spectacular, involving everything from spiritual presence, revelation knowledge, multiplication of food, physical healings, weather miracles, words of knowledge, etc., that to chalk them all up to delusions makes less sense than to acknowledge something distinctly peculiar must be happening.

When I exercise biblical faith, I am not working myself into an altered psychotic state to convince myself to trust Him with my heart while my mind is fighting it. I am not repeating omens or mantras to change my mind and convince myself to believe things that are not true. I am investing trust in someone I know is trustworthy. Trust based on evidence is what initial or saving faith is. Then, once we know someone, we can trust them even before they perform the action(s) we are trusting them for, which is what the Apostle Paul was referring to when he wrote that we "walk by faith, not by sight." (2 Corinthians 5:7 KJV).

Here is an example of this principle of trust based on evidence and experience, as practiced by the Lord Jesus Himself: When Jesus' cousin, John the Baptist, was in prison he called for two of his disciples to send word to Jesus and ask Him a very pointed question, "Are You the Expected One, or do we look for someone else?" (Luke 7:19). As many atheists define faith, Jesus' response was strange. He did not say, "Just tell John to have faith," or "Tell John to just believe and that is all the proof he will need." No, his response was to instruct John's disciples to go back to John and report the things He (Jesus) was doing and saying. He said, in effect, go share the evidence I am giving for Who I am. "Go and report to John what you have seen and heard: the blind receive sight, the lame walk, the lepers are cleansed, and the deaf hear, the dead are raised up, the poor have the gospel preached to them." (Luke 7:22b).

There is much more power in the actual words of Scripture than in all our arguments, logic, and reasoning. Whenever I have the liberty, I go to passages such as this story in Luke 7 and read (aloud) the passage to illustrate my point. The writer of Hebrews explains that "the word of God is living and active, and sharper than any two-edged sword, even penetrating as far as the division of soul and spirit, of both joints and marrow, and able to judge the thoughts and intentions of the heart." (Hebrews 4:12). Even when I am speaking to people who believe the Bible is fictitious, specious nonsense, I often use questions such as, "Do you mind if I read something from Scripture to explain how I arrived at this conclusion?" Acquiescing to this request is like agreeing to allow the placing of mental and spiritual explosives in the mind of the skeptic. The word is powerful, whether I think so or not.

In my experience, attention to reason and arguments, a friendly demeanor, genuine love, and a kind disposition are helpful, even mandatory, when sharing Christ with skeptics. But the word of God, with the Holy Spirit, may pierce through, arrest attention, and break hard hearts. Take care not to neglect these power resources in your witnessing encounters.

Jesus is still in the business of demonstrating and proving Himself to people who are open and receptive to the possibility that He is Who He claims to be. No one, whether an atheist or someone who already believes in God, can come to God on their terms, according to their preferences, pride intact, bringing God a list of demands both for how He must be and how they will come to Him. Thankfully, for those whose hearts are inclined toward the Lord, no one ever needs to worry that they just cannot have enough faith to become a Christian. He looks at the disposition—the heart—of any would-be follower and if He likes what He sees He deposits the right amount of faith for that person to find and accept His presence and Lordship. Above everything else, faith is a gift from Him. "For by grace you have been saved through faith; and that not of yourselves, it is the gift of God;" (Ephesians 2:8). Pray that the atheist or agnostic you know will begin to experience godly sorrow over their sin for, whether they realize it or not, this is a step toward God. Most atheists who repent and surrender to the Lord Jesus come step-by-step over a rather lengthy period. In many ways, converting from skepticism is like converting from another religion. They leave behind friends who refuse to understand their journey, habits that refuse to surrender easily, and thoughts and inclinations that, while being renewed may not yet be completely surrendered.

Without Christ, all lives are incredibly desperate and ultimately meaningless, but some people have just not realized that yet. Many skeptics are importing meaning by assuming, without warrant if there is no God, that their own lives *mean* something, can have a positive impact, or stand for some noble purpose larger than self. But without God, and the promise that we survive this life, there is no real purpose, because all of humanity winds up dead and forgotten in the heat death of the universe. People who do not trust in God, exercising faith toward Him are still exercising faith, but their faith is in their self-effort, or in the meaning(s) they are trying to import.

Faith is a Synonym for Gullibility

1. What's your biggest personal challenge right now, and why?

2. When we ask questions of our interlocutors, they help us shift the burden of proof, give us time to think and process, and convey a proper spirit of interest and discourse rather than lecture and sermonizing: What are some questions you might ask someone who believes Christians are guilty of being gullible and not thinking critically when it comes to faith?

3. What's your story? How did you initially know the truth of the gospel? How have grounds for that trust continued to be established in your life?

4. As you continue in this small group study you will learn many pieces of evidence which you may find helpful to share with skeptics. None of those pieces will be useful if you do not first establish a position that earns you the right to speak. Pray and ask the Lord to bring people to your awareness and lead you to be strategic in sharing Christ with them in the coming weeks. You may start with just one. Ask the Lord to lay a soul on your heart.

5. What could you do in the next seven days to help prepare the ground for your witness to this person?

Pray for one another, for the church or churches represented in your group, and for the souls of lost people clouded by atheism, agnosticism, and skepticism.

Chapter Four

Miracles Do Not Happen

The statement, "miracles do not happen," is another slogan atheists repeat. It is important to understand how someone can maintain this position despite what Christians believe is so much evidence to the contrary. This is especially true if you are a Pentecostal Christian. You may wonder how any sensible person can discount or deny miracles.

The reason atheistic slogans work is because they can help a person maintain plausible deniability about the work and witness of God. But the only way such slogans can remain powerful, to that effect, is if there are rational ways to appear to support them. In the case of the "no evidence for God" claim that support comes by redefining the word evidence.

But let us make an admission here. Some of the blame for this false claim about miracles lies at the feet of exaggerating Christians and charlatans who claim miracle status for events and circumstances for which it logically does not apply. Put another way, when everything is miraculous, *nothing* is. There is an undeniable proliferation of miracle claims which are dubious at best and fraudulent at worst. We do our cause a disservice when we pass them along or even tacitly endorse them by our silence.

Many Christians, marvelling at God's hand in His creation, truly do see nearly everything as miraculous, but that has the unintended consequence of rendering the definition of a miracle meaningless. If it is a "miracle," for example, when my aunt responds to the medication and surgery then atheists have a right to question why science should not receive most (they say all) of the credit, especially if a non-praying atheist is statistically just as likely to have a similar medical response. They are not, by the way, but that is beyond this volume. If every baby born is also a "miracle" then we have stretched the word "miracle" to the breaking point, and it no longer means anything at all.

This book and my diatribe will not likely fix any of those systemic issues in the body of Christ, but we still need to be able to help disabuse the skeptics in our lives of the notion that miracles do not happen for (at least) two especially important reasons: First, the denial of miracles is usually part of a larger denial of the supernatural in general. If I can demonstrate that the supernatural is genuine, I have helped my skeptical friend lose a plank in his platform of denying God. Second, the fulcrum, and central core of Christianity is the miraculous resurrection of the Lord Jesus from the dead. Some theologians go as far as to say that the only reason for the continued existence of miracles throughout history is to continue to corroborate and demonstrate the case for Christ. I do not go that far, but miracles are certainly a part of making that case. Historically, God has always used miracles and the miraculous to demonstrate and prove His case.

What is a miracle? That is a good question. . . and the answer is in dispute even among theologians and noted Christian thinkers. Professor John Lennox says it is when "the Creator intervenes in His own creation."[16] Traditionally a miracle has been defined as an event that supersedes or violates the laws of nature. A better definition is that a miracle is an extraordinary event, not explicable by natural or scientific laws, deemed to be the work of a divine agent.

Miracles, rather than "breaking" the laws of nature, demonstrate that those laws describe what happens with great regularity when God does not feed in new information, intervene, or obstruct the way things naturally work had He not interceded. Theoretically, for example, if a large enough wind machine could be built and powered, one could turn away a hurricane. God is simply big enough and powerful enough to resist and overcome the natural course of things.

Whichever definition one prefers it would seem the event has to be much more than just highly improbable to qualify as a real miracle. I am convinced an exceptionally fine reason why God does not always heal in answer to prayer is that if He did then miracles would be so common that they would fail to qualify as meaningful evidence of the Supernatural.

In many instances, atheists and agnostics would (likely) still not believe. They could assume, for example, that there is just something

---

[16] John Lennox, *Can Science Explain Everything?* (Charlotte, NC: The Good Book Co., 2019), 80.

about believing in miracles, etc. that causes the natural order to respond, by some mechanism yet undiscovered. They already make a similar argument when confronted with the life-changing behavioral results of trusting in Christ. They argue that belief in Him causes psychological change but that that belief still may not be grounded. i.e., belief itself may impact circumstances and brain chemistry, but not the imaginary God the belief is in.

So, what is the truth about miracles? Almost all Christians know that miracles happen, and the clear majority even believe they have experienced at least one. In a 1999 CBS News poll 59% of "extremely religious" Americans (25% of the population) said they believed they had seen or experienced a miracle.[17] When you think about it, if even one of the miracle claims is true—a very high likelihood as many of them are carefully documented, meticulously studied, and medically verified—then the claim that miracles do not happen fails.

I combat the claim by telling personal stories about miracles I have experienced and then I follow that with a question or two asking how I am supposed to make sense of my experience considering their assertion. Caution: If you do not have a legitimate miracle story – one that has no satisfactory natural explanation – do not use this tactic. Any atheist repeatedly indoctrinated with this slogan is adept at looking for every natural explanation, no matter how strained. So do not trot out the story of your healing from cancer if it followed rounds

---

[17] https://www.cbsnews.com/news/poll-do-you-believe-in-miracles/ retrieved 10/20/2022.

of chemo and major surgery. You are appropriately grateful for God's watch-care, and protection, and your story may, indeed, be a miracle, but it is not a slam dunk case for the miraculous intervention of God, except to you.

Thankfully there has also been some exceptionally good research done in the field of miracles. If, for some reason, my testimonies do not seem to have much impact, I ask a question: "How much academic research have you done in this area? You are certainly entitled to your opinion; do you have any studies or empirical data that suggest you're right?" I have never had this backfire on me, but there is a common response worth noting and worth arming yourself against.

A few "prayer studies" have been done which produced mixed results that atheists find encouraging. By that I mean such studies have rarely even purported to confirm, one way or another, whether prayer works. If you know anything about scientific methodology the reason will become clear. A rational person can also spot that clinging to these studies for support of one's position presents a classic case of confirmation bias.

Confirmation bias is rarely intentional. It is the practice of interpreting data and outcomes to support what you already believe. Since it is usually done on a subconscious level, Christians may be just as guilty of practicing it. It is almost always easier to spot in someone with whom you disagree than in yourself.

The biggest problem with a prayer study is building a reliable control group –i.e., a group of people not being prayed for during the study. There is simply no way to stop someone from praying for someone who is sick or in need of prayer. The group *not* receiving prayer may be receiving more prayer than the group intentionally receiving it. Who knows whether a distant aunt or relative is praying for a person in the control group? It is just an impossible study to do with serious scientific rigor or reliability.

Aside from the fact that scientists have no reliable ways to conduct prayer studies so that the results can (often) be interpreted to support either side of the miracle debate, there are two other problems with using or citing them: First, they are beside the point. To prove the atheist's claim to be false does not take a massive sampling or a double-blind test. If one verifiable miracle has ever happened, then strict naturalism fails and there is a supernatural component present in the universe. Second, the results of these studies, so far, have been a mixed bag. Some studies seem to show that prayer is effective while others, performed just as carefully, seem to show no effect whatsoever. The only way to use these studies would therefore be to "cherry pick," which is fallacious and would not contribute to the discovery of any underlying truth.

Duke University's Harold G. Koenig, M.D. says, "Studies have shown prayer can prevent people from getting sick — and when they do get sick, prayer can help them get better faster."[18] Hooray for our side!? Not so fast. Other studies seem to show little if any benefit, or even adverse responses to intercessory prayer.[19] These are, of course,

---

[18] https://spiritualityandhealth.duke.edu/index.php/harold-g-koenig-m-d retrieved 10/18/2022
[19] https://www.nytimes.com/2006/03/31/health/31pray.html retrieved 10/18/2022

the studies atheists prefer to site.

So, is it a wash, with neither side winning the day regarding miracles? Not hardly. Specific miracle claims have been studied, documented, and verified for centuries. A recent academic work detailing and outlining some of the most well-attested, medically verified ones is the two-volume study, *Miracles*, from Professor Craig Keener. It is an impressive collection and defense of not only miracles chronicled throughout history but also the overarching claim that such miracles support the interaction of divine agency – i.e., "God did it."

These kinds of studies matter because they are positive evidence *for* miracles. To rebut the slogan, "miracles do not happen," only requires sufficient evidence for one miracle. Of course, slogans need no rebuttal, but positive evidence does. As the famous atheist, the late Christopher Hitchens wrote, "That which can be asserted without evidence, can be dismissed without evidence."[20] You should remember his statement when confronted with unfounded, unsupported opinions.

Remember, one reason atheists are apt to reject miracles is that Christianity is founded on one – the bodily resurrection of the Lord Jesus. If that miracle happened, then Christianity is true. If Christianity is true, then God exists, and one can be accepted by Him only through personal identification with the Lord Jesus. Forgiveness of sin is only possible because of His death on the cross. Those are either t he most audacious and empty claims

---

[20] Christopher Hitchens, *God Is Not Great: How Religion Poisons Everything* (New York, NY: Twelve Books, 2007), 150.

ever made, or the best news the world has ever heard.

Christianity is no modest proposition, merely involving the attempted imitation of a well-lived life. Becoming a Christian starts with acknowledging my sin debt, a liability so large only God Himself could pay it. That admission pummels personal ego and pride but leads to something so valuable it is worth every humiliating blow. At the heart of the gospel is the acknowledgment that people are not spectacular and praiseworthy, but horribly broken and desperately in need of mercy, forgiveness, and redemption – a realization against which our natural flesh rebels.

As recorded in Galatians 3:24, the Apostle Paul wrote that the law of God is a schoolmaster, tutor, or guardian, set before us and written on our conscience to lead us to Christ and justification by faith. The just condemnation of living as a lawbreaker feels (emotionally) bad, draining, and even icky, and it's supposed to. People respond to pain in various ways. One common way is to ignore it. That is a reason many cancers aren't detected until they are stage 4 when it is too late to treat them.

Cancer is eventually undeniable, but not so a seared conscience. The longer someone ignores their conscience the easier it is to ignore. Then, when confronted with the reality that there will be an ultimate reckoning – there is a God to Whom we are accountable, that reminder brings back a conviction they are desperately trying to avoid. I am convinced that is often a reason atheists become so angry. A God Who does not exist cannot upset my applecart. Claims of a non-existent God should bother me no more than the threat that the tooth fairy will stop leaving money if I do not clean up my room.

Atheists rail against miracles and roundly reject them, especially the resurrection, because it forms the heart of the case demonstrating the truth of the gospel. So, ever since the beginning, within days, even hours of the resurrection, people wishing to escape its implications have been developing alternative theories to explain it away. They could even be successful if it were not for those annoying facts of history and the millions of testimonies of changed lives, miraculous interactions, interventions, and healings by Christ throughout two millennia. Dead men can leave a legacy, but Christ leaves an impact. He impacts people like only Someone alive and well can do. He is still saving everyone who sincerely calls on His name – a stubborn fact that refuses to conveniently die in the face of atheist dogma.

The resurrection is intrinsically linked with other miracles, because if other miracles can occur, then the resurrection, an event in the historically distant past, is at least possible. If someone rejects miracles in general, or out of hand, it is easy to see how no case, no matter how strong, could be persuasively made (to them) for the resurrection. On the other hand, if miracles are still occurring, then the resurrection may have also occurred. The resurrection is central to the core claims of Christianity. As the Apostle Paul wrote, "If Christ has not been raised, your faith is worthless; you are still in your sins." (I Corinthians 15:17). Writing as an atheist, the late Antony Flew, a brilliant philosopher, admitted, "Certainly, given some beliefs about God, the occurrence of the resurrection does become enormously more likely."[21]

Because of this connection, laying the foundation for acceptance of the resurrection frequently depends (apologetically) on making a case for more contemporary, documented, recorded, corroborated, verifiable miracles. Such an approach is difficult, and I have already warned you about categorizing the miraculous by the most stringent standards, especially when speaking with an atheist. And remember, you do not necessarily have to "succeed." The goal of each discussion is forward momentum and progress, not domination but disturbance. The Apostle charged us to give the reasons we believe, not to force our mindset on someone else (1 Peter 3:15).

When you are making progress, a hardened atheist will often respond that even though the case(s) you appeal to seem(s) miraculous we do not know everything, and a natural explanation is probably still more likely. Variations of that response appeal to other (currently) unidentified forces at work – almost anything but God will do – the fact that some conditions spontaneously reverse (more about that later), or that the people involved had motives for lying. Perhaps the most common response is to "cop out" completely. "I don't know how that happened, but it can't be God, because there's no evidence for God."

I hope it is not lost on you how circular this last response is. In the context of demonstrated/proven miracles, such a response begs the question. The case for God's existence is cumulative, and miracles are a part of it. We are making our cumulative case by marshaling all the

---

[21] In Habermas and Flew, *Did Jesus Rise from the Dead? The Resurrection Debate*, ed. Terry L. Miethe (San Francisco: Harper and Row, 1987), 39; cf. also 3, 49-50.

evidence in support of an overarching theory of the case. The theory that accounts for all the evidence in the least contrived or ad hoc way, should win. We make our case brick-by-brick, but the rebuttal, to be fair, cannot be made in the same way.

Why? Any single piece of evidence can be given a contrived context, suggesting it is not evidentiary, but when all (or a preponderance of) the pieces support the prosecution's theory, that too – the fact that the case theory coheres – must be accounted for. That is something atheists rarely (if ever) do. It is too painful. The case for miracles opens the possibility that strict empiricism is unwarranted, and the atheist's worldview is not only inaccurate but woefully inadequate.

Questions are your friends. Atheists do not have a more logical and rational explanation for documented contemporary miracles. The answer that makes the most sense, there is a God who intervenes from time to time, is the one from which they have been running. Depending on which miracle account is under consideration the questions will differ. Your goal must be to ask questions in a (relatively) non-threatening way, taking the emphasis off their response, so they will continue engaging and not feel attacked. I usually ask, "Given your view, that God doesn't exist, how should I be interpreting all of these facts, and this miracle, which suggests to me that He does?"

Now, what about "spontaneous remissions?" Don't they make it impossible to claim any reversal is the result of divine intervention? Not at all. Just like prayer studies cannot guarantee a "prayer-free" control group, we have no way of knowing whether someone's spontaneous remission was due to a merciful work of God. It is perfectly reasonable to affirm the hypothesis that God showed up with "healing in His wings" (Malachi 4:2). Given the cumulative case for God, that interpretation is better than any competing hypothesis.

Gary Habermas, a leading historical resurrection scholar, lays out a "minimal facts case" for the resurrection. His case posits that the best explanation, for a minimal set of facts on which most New Testament historians agree, is that God raised Jesus from the dead. His work on the resurrection is stellar, but his more daunting task (apologetically) is fighting the a priori dismissal of the evidence that refuses to point in (what atheists consider to be) the right direction. In his book, The Risen Jesus and Future Hope, he wrote a very helpful chapter confronting this task. This author heartily recommends the whole volume. In a chapter on A Theistic Universe, he makes a strong, scholarly case that "Scholars must not reject well-evidenced events simply because they do not fit their worldview."[22] But even without the premises which led to his conclusion, it seems appropriate to at least ask, "Do you think you may be rejecting well-evidenced events because they don't fit your worldview?" The truthful answer would almost certainly be "yes," but regardless of the answer, the question should make our skeptical friends do some necessary self-appraisal.

Thankfully, from time to time, despite our sinfulness, God intervenes in this fallen world and provides a miracle. One cannot count on a miracle to erase the consequences of years of bad personal

---

[22] Gary Habermas, *The Risen Jesus and Future Hope* (Boulder, CO, New York, NY: Rowman and Littlefield Publishers, 2003), 71.

health, financial, or relational choices, but occasionally, in His mercy, He will even do that. Many miracles are meticulously documented and provide the most plausible explanations for well-documented events. Even one miracle constitutes substantial evidence against naturalism. It is silly to insist that strict naturalism, or materialism accurately characterizes a world where miracles happen.

Miracles do not Happen

1. Take a few minutes to share personal miracle stories in your group. Most groups of at least three Christians have a story or two. Help one another evaluate the force of individual stories from the point of view of a skeptic. Be harsh, but fair. Remember: not everything miraculous can withstand critical scrutiny and constitutes good evidence *for* the miraculous. You may be a person who sees God's hand in almost everything – a true perspective, but perhaps not helpful when defending miracles. Can your group anticipate and practice dealing with objections to the story or stories you just shared?

2. Are you skeptical enough, too skeptical, or not skeptical enough when hearing a miracle testimony? Defend your answer and give an example if possible.

3. Discuss how you will personally handle the objection that "miracles do not happen." In your group, help one another refine their responses so that every member is ready to give a defense (1 Peter 3:15).

4. Is it normative Christianity for God to provide "miracles on-demand?" Why, or why not?

Close the meeting with prayer for one another.

Chapter Five

Extraordinary Claims Require Extraordinary Evidence

Carl Sagan may have been the first to utter this old canard.[23] Modern atheists have popularized it, but it certainly precedes them. Although "extraordinary" is obviously in the eye of the beholder, most atheists spout this slogan as if they have dropped the truth bomb to end all discussion. What it means is debatable but what they regularly mean by it is, "No matter what evidence you present, it will never be enough."

In a way, they are correct, because until they are open to the promptings and persuasion of God no argument will suffice to overcome their obstinate, stubborn resistance. These are not pejorative assessments. According to Christian theology all estranged humanity is fallen and rebellious toward God, whether outwardly— through paganism, atheism, Satanism, etc. or inwardly. Even those of us who know the Lord Jesus are in a constant battle with our fleshly

---

[23] On the 1980 TV series 'Cosmos', episode 12 (titled 'Encyclopedia Galactica')

natures and our first thoughts are often ego-centric—for self-aggrandizement, personal enrichment, etc.

Like so many atheist slogans this is not so much an argument as an assertion trying to masquerade as one. It would get you nowhere, but it would be perfectly valid for you to also assert that the very statement, "extraordinary claims require extraordinary evidence" is an extraordinary claim. Why? "Extraordinary" is notoriously difficult to precisely define. If the claim is extraordinary then, by their reasoning, they must have extraordinary evidence for it. But they don't. They have a disposition against God, so they are actively grasping for any pretense to reinforce it.

Once you see through the atheists' tendency to substitute meaningless slogans for critical thinking, reason, and evidence, it is easy for you to, at least, not be fooled by their twisted logic. That is the first step. You may not be able to refute it yet, but at least do not be fooled by it. Atheists who quote Sagan are not (intentionally) being disingenuous. They believe the statement is true, and they do not think you have any evidence that qualifies as extraordinary. Remember, many of them think you do not have evidence at all.

Forgetting, for the time being, that "extraordinary" is an arbitrary term, do extraordinary claims require extraordinary evidence? It sounds right, and often it is. But the statement sounds like we are setting up an iron-clad criteria by which we evaluate extraordinary claims. After all, the statement was not that "extraordinary claims sometimes require extraordinary evidence." Atheists certainly throw this claim around like it is a logical absolute, but if that is what they mean, it is demonstratively false.

Extraordinary and improbable events happen all the time, and most of the time we do not have extraordinary evidence for these events. We nevertheless do not doubt them, and we would lose much of history if we did. So, on a scale of 1 – 10, we must score this extraordinary claim a zero – a big swing and a miss, since it's asserting something as absolute and certain that is anything but.

Often cited examples are the conquests of Alexander the Great. Historians are in universal agreement that they happened. But we have no documentation until centuries afterward. Still, they consider such documentation, hundreds of years later, as sufficient to know what happened. Is the level of documentation extraordinary? Not particularly. So, by atheists reasoning such conquests never happened. Except they did. What that tells us is that the criteria are far too restrictive to be meaningful, or even useful.

Consider the resurrection, an event no atheist can believe is true. In my view, their oft-used slogan works against them. To disprove the resurrection, they must produce some rather extraordinary evidence that more plausibly explains the basic facts. It is beyond the scope of this book to review those facts, but such a task is a very tall order indeed. So, in the case of the resurrection, many skeptics are proposing responses to the evidence that are much more extraordinary than the admission that the most plausible explanation is that God raised Jesus from the dead.

I do not scoff at their desperate explanations, but honestly, all of them are laughable. When the only way to continue rejecting the resurrection is to posit something even more extraordinary than the resurrection, your theory is in trouble. In truth, none of the alternative natural explanations of the historical resurrection data make plausible sense of all the data. James D. G. Dunn summarizes: "Alternative interpretations of the data fail to provide a more satisfactory explanation."[24] Professor of Philosophy, Stephen Davis, of Claremont McKenna College, agrees that critics "are unable to come up with a coherent and plausible story that accounts for the evidence at hand. All of the alternative hypotheses with which I am familiar are historically weak; some are so weak that they collapse of their own weight once spelled out.... the alternative theories that have been proposed are not only weaker but far weaker at explaining the available historical evidence."[25]

By far the most fashionable way to historically deny the resurrection is to deny that a supernatural event can occur. As we have seen, that is called "question-begging," and it is a logical fallacy. Arguments for the resurrection are designed to prove the very thing being denied by that position. It should be easy to see that given no leeway to establish a single supernatural event, based on an a priori denial of such events, the resurrection cannot be established regardless of whether it is true.

The argument is sound, but the opposing criteria are not. That is like setting the beginning pieces of a chess game in checkmate rather

---

[24] James Dunn, *The Evidence for Jesus* (Louisville, KY: Westminster, 1985), 76.
[25] Stephen Davis, "Is Belief in the Resurrection Rational? A Response to Michael Martin," *Philo 2* (Spring–Summer 1999): 57–58.

than the standard neutral starting positions. Of course, you win, but you are cheating. We all know that cheaters never truly win. Such slogans are a lazy thinker's elixir. They sound good, and they help me fight a position I am philosophically opposed to, so they become my shortcut to stop the conversation without truly responding to any of the evidence. Despite the obvious flaws with this slogan, it has gotten great traction, both through constant repetition and the fact that it *sounds* so reasonable. Although it is not true it seems it should be.

As always, we should be giving answers and making our defense with gentleness and respect. A good way to start, when confronting this slogan, is by admitting the statement certainly sounds like a reasonable position to hold. There are some questions I find helpful: "Do you think that's true in every circumstance and for every subject? Could there be exceptions? Could there be something true, and for which there is evidence, but we simply do not have the knowledge to inspect that evidence? Shouldn't we always look for the best available evidence whether we consider it extraordinary or not?" The purpose of such questions is not just to avoid the friction of the conflict but to help your friend discover flaws and holes in her reasoning.

Now, here is a warning: good defense attorneys, so we are told, never ask a question to which they do not already know what answer will be given. But good Apologists often do, and the reason is simple. We are trying to win the hearts and minds of people, and questions are extremely helpful for people to find a change in perspective they can comfortably embrace as their own. When I ask, "Shouldn't we always look for the best *available* evidence whether or not we consider it extraordinary?" I frequently hear the response, "God knows what would convince me. If He exists but does not provide it, then He is an unfair God." Ouch! That charge is intuitively wrong, but it also "lands" in a way we are often not comfortable admitting. Even after you have taken the time to study it out, think it through, etc., and you have worked out a response, you should apply such a response very carefully, even sparingly, if at all.

Best case scenario: You dominate them mercilessly. They surrender. "You're right!" "UNCLE!" "I give up." "You win." They may even accept Christ, but human nature being what it is, there may always be a little something about you that unsettles them. That does not fit smoothly in the "win" column. No one should start their walk with Christ estranged from the person who led them to Him. Or worse, they could wind up being a disciple of your confrontational, "take no prisoners" methodology, and you have helped create another mean-spirited, dominating, un-Christlike "witness," another person not teaching people to "observe all things whatsoever I commanded you," (Matthew 28:20) and another person whose methods do not remotely resemble Christ's heart.

The adage is true that a person convinced against their will is of the same opinion still. As recorded in Isaiah 1:18, even the Lord invites us to come and reason together with Him. If the Lord chooses to reason with me, rather than to dominate me, should not I also choose that? When Christians decide it is better to verbally bludgeon someone with the truth, they are forgetting to cooperate with God in the way that He made us. It is difficult, and at times we find it nearly impossible, to resist setting someone straight about what to believe or how to think. But once you take that approach you are no longer cooperating with God, and you have taken the enemy's bait. Satan wants a confrontational, "winner take all" encounter between you and the skeptic. God wants a bride who willingly, and lovingly responds to His overtures.

Regardless of how tempting it is to laugh off this slogan, ridicule it, or even simply point out its obvious flaws, those responses are also not winning strategies. Remember, most skeptics, like people in general, are defensive and prideful, which can be a volatile combination. It is best to lead someone to a conclusion that becomes their own. People change their minds about God based on myriad pieces of evidence, processed through the prism of their life experiences, and filtered through varying expectations.

The most helpful thing you can do is set personal passion and pride aside, and simply reason, question, and affirm your skeptical inquirer. Affirm? Yes. Affirm and accept them when they tell you why they think the way they do. Affirm them by also helping them see their questions and answers from an altered perspective.

At first blush, the "extraordinary claims" slogan seems like a strong and effective rebuke. Once it is exposed it is almost laughable. But please, do not laugh. When I have responded to it sarcastically, or by pointing out how silly it is, that has never been a helpful or winning tactic. I have never met an atheist who has been impressed with or won over by that approach.

The slogan, "extraordinary claims require extraordinary

evidence," or a derivation of it, is a one-size-fits-all response from atheists. When I hear it, I am aware that whatever area of apologetics we may be discussing, the person I am speaking with has run out of argumentative gas. It is quite often indicative of the fact that they can no longer refute my arguments and have now devolved to merely mocking them or claiming even though they succeed they are not "extraordinary" enough.

Once they have said it, and after I have tried to help them rethink their position about it, I have often used a form of this final question: "I am sure we both agree that 'extraordinary' is in the eye of the beholder but why do you think it is extraordinary enough to convince many of the world's top scientists and greatest thinkers, but not sufficient to warrant your study or attention?" I am carefully asking this question with true curiosity and interest and with a caring demeanor. Your tone is vitally important. Do not ask this in a text message. Change it to suit your discussion – for example, if they say they have studied it carefully alter the ending of it – but do not leave it unasked. Even if asked rhetorically it can be a powerful "leave behind" for the Spirit to continue to bring back to their attention.

Atheists think they will be giving something up to follow Christ. They are right. It is painfully difficult to convince someone that "losing yourself is the only true way to find yourself." Think of how that would sound to you if you had spent your entire adult life believing slogans and unfounded assertions to avoid and blunt the witness of the Spirit. Perhaps you did. But whether you did or did not, you must find space and resonance within yourself to remember and honor the soul-searching changes you went through on your path to God and give your atheist friends the courtesy of traveling their path without you throwing up unnecessary roadblocks.

They are not yet aware of your amazing discovery, that the Lord Jesus is the pearl of great price (Matthew 13:46). Their novel way of denying Him notwithstanding, they are still precious souls for whom He died. Even if they become angry, insulting, and petty, as much as they would like you to, don't lose your cool and forget that fact. Lost is lost. They are no more lost than the man who grew up in church but decided to reject the Christ He knows is the Way, Truth, and Life.

Claims, extraordinary or not, simply require a sufficient warrant to demonstrate they are true. The cumulative case that the Christian worldview is accurate is formidable. I would even call it extraordinary, but that word is not precise enough to be meaningfully used in this context. There is a cumulative preponderance of evidence from several fields and disciplines, throughout society, history, culture, science, and philosophy that lead most plausibly to the conclusion that Jesus is Who He says He is and that through Him we find our truest and most noble purpose. That is extraordinary to me, but more importantly, it is more than sufficient to make the case that, at a bare minimum, He lives!

It is beyond the scope of this book to provide that evidence in any detail, but it is provided by the authors in the books I have listed in the Bibliography. Ironically, many atheists will look for it here, where it is not present, and accuse me of lying about or merely asserting my positions. Not all of them will because those who read carefully understand that I am under no obligation to make a case in a book where I have briefly but carefully laid out the reasons (evidence) for why I believe as I do regarding the narrow topic of atheism's silly beliefs.

As an aside, that is one reason to avoid online comment sections and chat rooms. If you do not want to explain, top to bottom, in excruciating detail, all the reasons for your entire cumulative case, be prepared to be accused of lying. It is a lazy but common accusation, often made to sidestep giving serious thought to your point of view. If you do not enjoy being accused of lying, whatever else you do, do not return the favor. Assume the person you are talking to is expressing what they believe is true.

Ironically, many atheists would rather use a slogan than provide any evidence that their worldview is correct, even a slogan such as, "extraordinary claims require extraordinary evidence," without providing any evidence that their slogan is in any way true.

One thing I know that is truly extraordinary is the extraordinary love of the Lord Jesus for me and every other fallen sinner. He left the splendor, glory, and majesty of heaven to live in the relative garbage heap of first-century Palestine and to lead a sinless, perfect, sacrificial life so that I could be redeemed, bought back, and placed in the family of God. Extraordinary is not nearly a big enough word.

Extraordinary Claims Require Extraordinary Evidence

1. Do you have a pain you're ignoring, a sin you're not confessing, or a burden you're not sharing? Risk trusting the group and unloading tonight.

2. Pray for skeptical friends, family, and strangers who refuse to see the evidence for Christ. Ask the Lord to help you be a conduit of His love and grace and an ambassador of His Kingdom in kind and loving ways.

3. Individuals in the group should finish this sentence: One thing that stood out to me in this chapter was _____. Go further and tell why.

4. Atheists will say that they are not taking a positive position that "God does not exist," yet this statement, "Extraordinary claims require extraordinary evidence," is making a claim, of sorts that at least implies that if a different kind of evidence were given then that person would give God more consideration. Do you think this statement is a cry for more evidence or a smokescreen to dismiss evidence? Why, or why not?

6. Do you know someone whom you believe is not surrendering to Christ because of the cost they are thinking it will require of them? How would you communicate persuasively and passionately with such a person?

7. Unfortunately, since this statement is a slogan and not an argument, people who use it sometimes take a condescending tone. So that you will not respond in kind and will be able to continue the

conversation prayer and the leadership of the Spirit become critical when witnessing to someone with that tone. If someone in your group is very familiar with atheists' retorts and statements, you might want to role-play a witnessing encounter and practice kind, measured responses.

End your meeting with prayer for one another, and prayers for any absent group members. Pray for skeptics known by members of your group.

Chapter Six

Everything Was Created
by Nothing

To be fair, atheists rarely (if ever) utter this exact statement. It is, however, the statement that most logically coheres to their worldview. For strict materialism to be true one must believe that not just plants and animals were the result of random mutations and non-guided processes, but the entire universe, in its strategic balance and exquisite beauty, was an accident, without an architect, designer, or design. In the long history of mankind, there was a brief period when that was not so hard to imagine. But today, with what we can empirically verify and observe about both the beginning of the universe and the incredibly precise fine-tuning of it, such a thought is impossible to rationally maintain.

On the opening page of Professor Lennox's website, he makes an incredibly telling statement: "Either human intelligence ultimately owes its origin to mindless matter; or there is a Creator. It is strange that some people claim that it is their intelligence that leads them to prefer the first to the second."[26] He ought to know. He has spent decades working with, conversing, and debating with some of the brightest, most celebrated scientists in the world, not only as their peer but often as their philosophical adversary.

Atheist astronomers and cosmologists write lengthy books and articles trying to detail how nothing became everything, something they would likely consider a scientific absurdity if not for the supernatural implications involved in the more well-reasoned alternative, that the apparent design and very existence of the universe is due to it having been designed and created. Some of them have admitted the obvious implications. The late Sir Frederick Hoyle, an English astronomer who formulated the theory of stellar nucleosynthesis is often quoted in this regard, although he was an avowed atheist. While studying enzyme development with Chandra Wickramasinghe, originally an agnostic on the issue of God, both admitted that, scientifically, it certainly appears "life was assembled by an intelligence." They further stated, "Indeed, such a theory is so obvious that one wonders why it is not widely accepted as being self-evident. The reasons are psychological rather than scientific."[27]

Like all scientific communities, the world of cosmology has its fair share of atheists, men and women who, despite such strong implications, work very hard to posit and develop completely natural

---

[26] Home page, JohnLennox.org, retrieved 10/24/2022.

[27] Sir Fred Hoyle and Chandra Wickramasinghe, *Evolution from Space: A Theory of Cosmic Creationism* (New York, NY: Simon and Schuster, 1981), chap. 9, "Convergence to God," esp. 130.

explanations—which arguably is, after all, the job of science. Scientists are not able to study anything but the natural world. It is all to which they have access. That does not mandate, however, that they refuse to notice when their empiricism points to something beyond nature. Professor John Lennox maintains that "it is atheism to which science gives little support."[28]

In fairness, not all cosmologists and astronomers who espouse such positions are non-believers. Many of them see the role of science as providing whatever natural and material explanations may be found and therefore simply rule out "God did it," as scientifically lazy and, perhaps more importantly, outside the realm of empirical investigation. Some of those same scientists freely admit that, while God cannot be studied empirically, the natural world appears to give secondary evidence, as the *effect* of His *cause*. Astronomer Owen Gingrich, professor emeritus of astronomy and of the history of science at Harvard University, stated flatly, "Compared to the human brain, stars are utterly trivial. So there are empirical reasons to suppose that the universe was designed and created for us."[29]

The scientific "status quo" is still a commitment to purely naturalistic explanations. But is such an a priori commitment to a naturalistic explanation the best approach for arriving at truth? Not if God did, indeed, design and create the universe. There is a strong

---

[28] John Lennox, *Can Science Explain Everything?* (Charlotte, NC: The Good Book Co., 2019), 18.
[29] Owen Gingrich, "Where in the World is God?" in *Man and Creation: Perspectives on Science and Theology,* ed. Michael Bauman (Hillsdale, MI: Hillsdale College Press, 1993), 219-20.

cumulative case that He did. That case is made several ways, but it often includes what philosophers of religion refer to as the "Kalam Cosmological Argument."

Stated briefly it is as follows: Premise 1: Everything that begins to exist has a cause for its existence. Premise 2: The universe began to exist. Conclusion: Therefore, the universe has a cause. In other words, the universe is not uncaused and is simply a brute fact. It requires a sufficient explanation to account for its existence. Science, rationality, and reason demand it.

From that conclusion, we perform a conceptual analysis which further concludes that God is the most reasonable Candidate for being the Cause of the universe. I will get to that in a few paragraphs, but for now let us consider the likelihood that the argument itself succeeds, since, as an inductive argument, if the premises are more plausibly sound than not the conclusion follows necessarily.

The first premise, that everything that begins to exist has a cause is also known as the law of contingency, a concept we have already touched on. It states something empirically certain, to the degree any fact can be. We know of nothing that exists that does not appear to be contingent, or that did not come from something else and that includes every planet, moon, star, land mass, creature, person, and thing. All material things, from all that we can observe, are contingent things; all beings, all matter, all the "stuff" of the universe.

That fact does not keep atheists from arguing about it. They realize there is an eventual supernatural implication in the cosmological argument, so they argue absurdities and non-sequiturs in their futile attempt to refute one or both of its premises. If atheists have a favorite slogan when it comes to logical arguments, it is to claim, without a smidge of evidence, "that argument has been completely debunked." It is important to remember that disagreement with an argument does not constitute rebuttal. Sometimes I say, "It better be, because if it's true then atheism is obviously untrue, wouldn't you agree?" The "debunked" slogan is supposed to be a conversation stopper, and I am doing whatever I can to keep the conversation flowing.

To be prepared with your own meaningful and substantive rebuttals you must acquaint yourself with the argument in more detail, using many of the resources referenced in the Bibliography of this volume. William Lane Craig has been defending this argument in debates, print, and peer-reviewed journals for decades, and in that time, he has substantively answered every objection brought against it. In my experience, premise one gets the most pushback, often starting with the question, "What do you mean by 'begins to exist?'" It is, nevertheless, a premise with strong support, both philosophically and scientifically.

Philosophically there must have been a beginning to the universe because an actual infinite cannot exist. Infinity is a useful term in mathematics, but all material things, including the universe, and time itself, must have a finite beginning and cannot exist eternally into the past. As philosopher and theologian Dr. Gary Habermas notes:

To indicate the unreasonable repercussions involved in accepting the existence of an actual infinite, several antinomies are often presented. A favorite involves the example of a library that contains an actual infinite number of books, each of them colored either red or black. In such a scenario, there would be as many black books as black and red books combined! Or again, the red books could all be withdrawn without altering the total number of volumes present![30]

A popular workaround, for the quandary of a universe that began to exist, is a multi-verse theory, postulating that universes die and give rise to another, sort of undulating in successive expansions and contractions over eons of time. This does not escape the philosophical objection that no material thing, including undulating universes, can be past eternal, nor does it even begin to touch on the teleological argument, not elaborated on in this volume, that the universe we inhabit seems meticulously designed for us, in hundreds of specific, measurable ways, within very close tolerances, exquisitely "fine-tuned" for our arrival and survival.

As for premise two, that the universe began to exist, that too is one of the most well-established facts of cosmology, but this has not always been the case. For many years, the "steady state" theory ruled the day in the study of origins. It was thought that the universe was eternal and consequently needed no explanation for its beginning. For all of eternity, the universe had just existed, with no need to argue

---

[30] Gary Habermas, *The Risen Jesus and Future Hope* (New York, NY: Rowman and Littlefield, 2003), 56.

how it began since it was assumed it never had begun. Today, it would not be an overstatement to say that virtually every reputable scientist who studies origins favors some sort of "Big Bang" cosmology. In other words, they uniformly agree the universe began to exist.

Remember, the universe includes all matter, space, energy, and time. So, while it is very hard for time-based beings (such as we are) to understand, before (causally not temporally) the universe began there was no matter to make it with, no time to make it in, no energy to make it with, and no space in which to put it.

And that brings me to the conceptual analysis I mentioned a few paragraphs back. If matter did not exist before the Big Bang event, then whatever is responsible for causing the universe is not made of matter. Similarly, if time did not exist before the Big Bang, then whatever the cause of the universe is must exist, in some way, outside of time, or perhaps timelessly. Since the universe encompasses all the known elements, space, and time then whatever created the "BANG" that started it all must be immensely powerful. We can further reason that because the explosion of the "bang" created meticulous order, symmetry, beauty, and even life itself rather than the chaos of all other explosions, whatever caused it had the capacity to reason and to think. The Big Bang seems planned to create rather than destroy, which is the opposite of what explosions usually do.

NOTE: It is now common to state that all existing matter was condensed into a single point – the "singularity," which exploded and eventually resulted in all the matter in the known universe. Despite decades of experimentation, we have no known mechanism whereby all that matter could be so compressed. Many good people are working on it. The Bible teaches something which, despite being very difficult to understand, seems to comport better with the known facts of science – creation from nothing. God required no raw materials to create everything that exists in the universe.

There are further ways to analyze the implications of the Kalam Cosmological Argument, which I will leave you to discover as you research outside of these pages. But think about what is already inferred from the evidence. Whatever caused the Big Bang that created the entire universe is space-less, timeless, immaterial, immensely powerful, and incredibly intelligent. Does that sound like anyone you know? I hope so, at least if you have a relationship with God.

This is such a strong argument that it draws the ire and the fire of many atheists and skeptics, but it is untouched by their best efforts. Dealing with all their objections is beyond the scope of this volume, but here are a couple of the most popular:

1. "You have not proven God because He would violate premise one, 'Whatever begins to exist has a cause.' Therefore, your argument fails unless or until you can answer the question, 'What caused God?'" I hear that one at least eight out of ten times when I share the cosmological argument. Perhaps the greatest living defender of the Kalam Cosmological Argument is Dr. William Lane Craig, a philosopher, author, and seminary professor. He answers this rebuttal attempt quite convincingly in several of his books and articles. I urge

you to consult them comprehensively.

Is it true that for an explanation to be valid, I must also have an explanation of the explanation? If God is credibly posited as the most reasonable inference from the data on hand, do I need to withhold my analysis unless I can also explain where God came from? It seems not, in this case. Here is why: We are only able to explore, observe, and investigate features and attributes of our physical universe. A necessary condition if God is the Cause of the universe (our laboratory), is for Him to exist, as analyzed, outside of the scope or bounds of our empirical investigation. We can only go back to the point when time began within the physical world. Put another way, God is like the Author of a novel. The characters in that novel, if given free will, could logically deduce His existence but never empirically investigate where He came from.

In addition, the demand that I provide not only the explanation (God), but the explanation of the explanation (where God comes from) breaks the bounds of logic, since it would then be necessary to explain that explanation, and so on in an infinite regression.

2. "Even if the argument is true, you are far from proving that the cause of the universe is God."

The people making this claim apparently do not realize that the argument does not end before the conceptual analysis is completed. They think the whole argument just proves the universe has a cause. Sometimes they speculate that the cause could be literally (or almost) anything since our knowledge only goes back as far as the explosion of the cosmic singularity that started the process. They may assert,

"We do not have any meaningful way to speculate prior (causally not temporally) to that explosion."

A philosophically unsophisticated atheist may view our hypothesis as a case of "special pleading," which is a logical fallacy that exempts the answer you postulate from the normal rigor and reasoning of thorough investigation. They are wrong about this objection. One reason is that the God hypothesis was established as the most likely inference *from* the information we have. We can speculate on what we do not have, but the best reasoning and science is observational, not speculative. Whatever the cause was, from all of the currently available facts, it shares many, and perhaps all of the attributes in common with how Christians view God from their Scriptures. That is intellectually and factually undeniable.

If there was a more plausible explanation, Christians would need to account for it with sufficient and credible reasons. We would be compelled to explain why it does not threaten our worldview. Atheists should have the same burden of proof when the most credible inference is to a Cause which, for all the world appears to be God.

So far, their alternative explanation, that everything was caused by nothing, or that the universe itself is the single uncaused thing, strains credulity and is almost certainly invalid, based on the science. That is why I categorize the notion as a "silly thing." Something as large as the universe, which comprises all known matter, space, time, and energy, and appears entirely composed of contingent things, cries out for an explanation. It is, of course, a goal of many scientists to find those explanations, but much to the dismay of supernatural skeptics in their ranks, those explanations regularly support the notion of a superintending agent – God.

To atheists, the universe presents more than merely the problem of its existence. It also appears to be incredibly "fine-tuned," something that, on atheism, one would not expect. By the second law of thermodynamics, it would not be expected. Yet there is almost universal agreement that the entire universe is incredibly fine-tuned, especially for the flourishing and maintenance of carbon-based life forms, i.e., human beings.

On atheism, such seeming intentionality makes no sense. It is, however, exactly what one would expect if theism were true. We are the crown of God's creation—made in His image, to be in an eternal relationship with Him. Everything else He made was the wind-up leading to humanity. In such a large universe that may sound incredibly vain, but it also appears to be true.

Everything Was Created by Nothing

1. On your personal prayer list, who do you wish you prayed for more often, and why?

2. The great soul-winner, Ray Comfort, often asked atheists, "Do you believe the unscientific statement that nothing created everything?" As a group, brainstorm some other ways to introduce the cosmological argument naturally into a witnessing opportunity.

3. Often the best way to combat strict naturalism, which this claim is an aspect of, is to live a life that is highly connected to God. In turn, as directed by the Spirit, convey personal testimonies of how someone else's life helped lead you to Christ.

4. Even in the Christian community there are different views on "Big Bang" cosmology, with some Christians going so far as to reject it based on their understanding of where the Genesis creation should fall on the timeline of the history of the universe and the creation of planet Earth. Considering the following factors try to reason through to a harmonious position:

   a. The timelessness of God – an eternal Being.

   b. In the Hebrew way of thinking, the construction is the son of Y" does not always mean a literal father/son relationship.

   c. The Hebrew word (Yom) used for day in the first chapter of Genesis can mean long periods of time. Furthermore, the sun and moon were not created until day four of the creation week. How long were "days" before solar (24-hour) days existed?

5.   Sometimes atheists go to great lengths to protect their beliefs in concepts and principles that appear to defy common sense and logic. Their rebuttals to the Kalam Cosmological Argument often seem to be particularly obtuse and illogical. Consider the common objections raised in the chapter and others you might think of and talk about how you might respond in ways that are respectful and helpful.

Close with prayer for one another – for consistency of life and witness, for victory over sin and the devil, and a dutiful and obedient response to 2 Timothy 2:15, "Be diligent to present yourself approved to God as a workman who does not need to be ashamed, accurately handling the word of truth."

Chapter Seven

Your God Endorses Slavery

You cannot be a defender of the Christian faith for long without running headlong into this issue, and especially instructions, which appear to be from God, about slavery, which include being able to beat fellow human beings, so long as they don't die, keep someone else's wife and children as your slaves for life, even after the husband slave has been freed, and other orders and admonitions that not only offend modern sensibilities but, if we're honest, seem to upend much of what we assume to be integral to the character and nature of God. Quite often, I am specifically asked about Exodus 21, though there are also other operative passages.

The first rule of hermeneutics (interpretation of texts) is context. Some would say it's also rules 2 and 3. Context is more than merely looking at the surrounding Scriptures - placing a text in its immediate textual context. It's also doing the hard work of understanding, as best we can, the historical milieu, the cultural background, and biblical interpretation also entails the process of developing an appreciation for what the text meant to the original intended recipients.

Scripture was written primarily, or on the first order, for those who read it first. We glean from it, by extension, but all of it, while still applicable to us, is not always applicable to us in the same ways as it was to its original audience. We do best when we ferret out what it meant to them and then apply it (in principle) to ourselves. That is not always an easy task.

Not every Christian reader is willing to do the hard work of digging into the cultural/historical contexts of the passages they read. Even more so, the average atheist is unlikely to have given (so-called) problem passages of Scripture much of a fair shake. As a result, many non-discerning readers of Scripture, particularly the Old Testament, have developed erroneous and errant views of its content, even for some passages where the meaning seems crystal clear.

They are often particularly prone to characterize God as morally flawed, or a mere projection of those who perceived themselves to be His followers. Since humanity has been evolutionarily growing in morality, it is no wonder God, Who (on Christianity) should be morally perfect, is often portrayed (especially in the Old Testament) as anything but. This, they say, gives them ample pause and sufficient reason to discount His existence, or, at the very least, the existence of the Hebrew God, Jehovah.

Unfortunately, much of the problem may boil down to an all too human tendency to not consider the vast differences in contexts between the cultures we are living in and the ones we are reading about. It is not merely that the language is not our own, but the land, people, and culture are so different from ours that we can easily misconstrue and misunderstand the authorial intent, and the instructions from God contained therein.

All that is not to say that the average reader cannot glean and learn from Scripture, especially as illuminated by the Holy Spirit, but a skeptic does not have the advantage of Supernatural insight. If it is important for Christians to consider multiple kinds of contexts, it is certainly important for atheists to as well. It often seems like atheist readers are willing to ignore context and any other principles of hermeneutics which interfere with their forgone conclusion, that God is a moral despot. Far too often, atheist readers are quick to criticize and painfully slow to comprehend. Doctors E. Randolph Richards and Brandon J. O'Brien, writing about hermeneutics in general, elaborate:

> We can easily forget that Scripture is a foreign land and that reading the Bible is a cross-cultural experience. To open the Word of God is to step into a strange world where things are very unlike our own   We don't know the geography or the customs or what behaviors are considered rude or polite. . .. we tend to read Scripture in. a way that makes sense on our terms. But there's no way around the fact that our cultural and historical contexts supply us with habits of mind that lead us to read the Bible differently than Christians in other cultural and historical contexts.[31]

To the point: I think a contextual understanding of Exodus 21 keeps our picture of the nature and character of God intact. Within the

---

[31] E Randolph Richards and Brandon J. O'Brien, *Misreading Scripture with Western Eyes* (Downers Grove, IL, IVP Books, 2012), 11.

immediate context of the chapter and the background information of Hebrew history, it is important first to understand that the "slavery" identified in Exodus 21 is not "chattel" slavery, such as that practiced in the United States before the emancipation proclamation. Instead, the slavery under discussion is a form of indentured servitude – an agreement into which both parties entered voluntarily for their mutual benefit.

Our modern sensibilities still do not like it, and we would much prefer the Bible refer to it in more palatable prose, but it was like antebellum slavery in name only. It was much more like the kind of slavery many of the first immigrants to the British colonies employed. The fare for travel to the new world was so cost-prohibitive that one-half to two-thirds of the immigrants to Britain's colonies came (initially) as indentured servants.[32] Those servants were overwhelmingly white. I mention that fact because any defense of any kind of slavery, even for different people, in different circumstances and different times, is often responded to with cries of "racism." It is increasingly difficult to simply relay facts without someone leveling such a charge – which they often design to shut you up.

If there is one person who has done the most study about slavery in the ancient world it may be classicists Peter Garnsey. In his carefully researched study of the slavery practiced in the cultures surrounding the Hebrews during the time Hebrews themselves practiced indentured servitude. He writes:

---

[32] David W. Galenson, "Indentured Servitude," in *The Oxford Companion to American History* (New York, NY: Oxford University Press, 2001), 368-69.

In the ancient world (and beyond), chattel (or property) s l a v e r y had three characteristics:
1. A slave was property.
2. The slave owner's rights over the slave's person and work were total and absolute.
3. The slave was stripped of his identity–racial, familial, social, marital.[33]

Theologian Paul Copan, who has copiously studied questions relating to God's supposed lack of personal morality wrote about Garnsey's findings:

> This doesn't describe the Hebrew servant at all, nor does it fit the non-Israelite slave in Israel. Israel's servant laws were concerned about controlling or regulating – not idealizing – an inferior work arrangement. Israelite servitude was induced by poverty. . .. entered into voluntarily, and . . .. far from optimal [but] the intent of these laws was to combat potential abuses, not to institutionalize servitude.[34]

But still, how could a loving God ever find justification for one man "owning," or especially beating another? Again, context is important. Jews today, are approximately 2/10 of 1% of the world's population. Yet for reasons known only to Him, Jews were the people God chose to make His own, to strike a covenant with, and to display

---

[33] Peter Garnsey, *Ideas of Slavery from Aristotle to Augustine* (Cambridge: Cambridge University Press, 1996), 1.
[34] Paul Copan, *Is God a Moral Monster?: Making Sense of the Old Testament God* (Grand Rapids, MI: Baker Books, 2011), 127.

to the larger world, through them, His power and love. The Old Testament gives several explicit and implicit examples of God allowing His people to do things that He neither ordains nor approves of. One example that comes to mind is when He gave them an earthly king (Saul), against His own will and counsel, because they clamored for one, to be like the nations surrounding them.

This author is not suggesting that God was indulgent with His chosen people. Any careful reading of the Old or New Testaments leads to a contrary conclusion. But the children of Israel were/are *peculiar* and *unique* to His plans. How He worked with them, and what He did to, or through them were often not indicative of the normal or usual ways He instructed them to behave. For example, the same God Who would eventually enshrine "Thou shalt not murder" as universal law, instructed Abraham to slay His own son, Isaac. If you're reading this volume and do not know how that turned out, please close the book, put it away, and choose a small group on basic Bible stories you would like to attend.

He, as the Author of life, Rewarder of the faithful, Judge, and Ruler over all of creation was/is free to choose, or not choose any people and free to use them to punish, instruct, lift, or humiliate any other person or group of people, since all of them were/are His creation. He did not need to check first with any of them to see how they may feel about it, nor does He need to check with any of us, living centuries later, to see whether His actions meet with our approval. Even if one has no further insight than that He exists and is God, He is under no obligation to explain Himself to His creatures.

All that is of first importance, because as we have seen, and will continue to see, the evidence that He exists is quite good. He does, in fact, also appear to be the God of the Old Testament, since the Man Who rose from the dead came preaching and representing that God and not some other god. The Lord Jesus was the single most likely candidate among all people who have ever lived, to know about and speak for God. Ironically, this is a fact often admitted even by those who are not His followers.

Logically, one must separate whether there is a God from the question of whether they like Him, approve of Him, or would surrender to Him. It should also be separated, to the degree possible, from whether you understand His priorities, processes, and plans. It should not be about whether you would respond like He does, or doesn't, or whether you approve or disapprove of Him. The question of *what* you think of Him is separate from the question of *whether* He exists. It is not unimportant, but it is (necessarily) not connected.

Nevertheless, we struggle and desire to make more sense of some Old Testament passages, especially considering what we learn about God through Christ in the pages of the New Testament. In His love and wisdom, ample and sufficient information about the ancient Near Eastern world is available to anyone truly seeking understanding, and not just looking for an opportunity to indict. When our picture is filled in by the missing cultural and historical context, and one considers that God does not normally interfere in the regular course of human cultural and civic development, a more charitable picture emerges.

Slavery, of the sort described in Exodus 21 and far worse, was a rampant and normal condition in the ancient Near Eastern world. It may have even been a necessary condition for the bare survival of many of the people involved, and it was most likely mutually beneficial in most cases. Consider this comparison. Today we have a somewhat broken, but robust criminal justice system. If one man agrees to perform a service for another but then reneges, a range of options are open to enforce compliance based on the terms of the contractual obligations. No doubt, in the future, some of those options will appear to have been barbaric. In our own recent history – just a little over one hundred years ago, repeat offenders were sometimes placed in stocks and bonds in the public square and deadbeats went to "debtor's prison." Both acts were part of the course of human development but are now considered deplorable. Still, historically speaking, they were not long ago.

As for "beating" someone – that too was practiced and still is in many parts of the world. It offends me but seems to be an extremely effective behavioral adjustment tool. Ironically, I'm also offended when parents refuse to discipline their children and allow them to be out of control and disrespectful. I guess I would need a little more context, and perhaps as importantly I would need to know what a "beating" entailed. In the case of a Master/Slave relationship, in the days of the Exodus, I am sure, based upon the broader context, that God expected other options to be exhausted before someone took the drastic step of "beating" a slave. So, when the slave was beaten it was expected to be a last resort.

Further, the master in the relationship was expected to provide, food, clothing, shelter, rest, and certain amenities as part of the contract. If a slave refused to fulfill their part, there were very few remedies available to the master. Jailing the errant slave, who had voluntarily agreed to the arrangement, ensured that all the expenses continued while the benefit was still not derived. Hence confinement offered no equitable solution for the owner. When "beating" was on the table (as a viable option) it probably, frankly, seldom ever had to be practiced. I got paddled one time, in the eighth grade, and learned immediately that compliance with a teacher's orders was much preferred and far less painful.

I think, considering the direction God was leading, the example of the Lord Jesus, and the testimony of the early church, that it is a mistake to flatly say, "God endorsed slavery and the beating of slaves." More accurately, he endorsed a system of equity where one could be indentured for a time and expected to perform services commensurate with that servitude. He also endorsed punitive measures to assure the mutual equity of all parties involved. However, guidelines and limits were placed on punishment methods.

If an owner/master was so harsh that he caused real harm to the slave the owner himself was punished by law, even to the point of death if the owner killed the slave. Since beating is not an exact science, these provisions in the law no doubt served to moderate the owner's behavior. Copan writes, "Are these Exodus laws perfect, universal ones for all people? No, but in this and other aspects, we continually come across improved legislation for Israelite society in contrast to surrounding ancient Near Eastern cultures."[35] In other words, all these accommodations seem to be vast improvements on slavery as practiced throughout the rest of the ancient Near Eastern world. If anything, such knowledge should force an honest skeptic to wonder how/why this one small group of people, unaided by a non-existent god, could live their lives so remarkably superior to every other culture of their time and geography. Skeptics seldom do that. It is almost as if the "god of this world" has them blinded.

Now, one who does not "factor in" human nature and does not have a robust comprehension of God's respect for free will, may still question; if God is real, why didn't he demand His people just not practice slavery at all? Why did God not dramatically change their circumstances so that all His people would have plenty without needing to resort to servitude? Those are good, and fair questions.

A better question might be, knowing human nature, and respecting free will, was God more loving and kinder to both slaves and owners by issuing guidelines and rules for the practice they were determined to participate in? Still, another question could be, considering the harsh realities of their day-to-day existence, what specific options could God have used, other than servitude, to ensure their continued growth and development, financial and life stability, which also did not violate their free will? As for the nature of those conditions, those conditions appear to have worked, at least if God's quest involved creating resilient, dependable, savvy people. Jewish

---

[35] Paul Copan, *Is God a Moral Monster? Making Sense of the Old Testament God* (Grand Rapids, MI: Baker Books, 2011), 136.

people, which such a low percentage of the world's population, have currently won about 20% of all Nobel prizes ever awarded.[36]

We certainly have Scriptural support for the idea that God likely acquiesced to their broken condition with a redemptive allowance of a flawed practice, including the Lord Jesus Himself Who, regarding divorce and remarriage said, "Moses wrote this command only as a concession to your hardhearted ways. In the original creation, God made male and female to be together. Because of this, a man leaves father and mother, and in marriage he becomes one flesh with a woman—no longer two individuals but forming a new unity." Mark 10:5-8 (The Message).

Now, what about that part where a slave marries someone while serving his tenure and then doesn't get to keep them when he leaves? It may be too much to ask our skeptical friends to apply a bit of logic. If I am dead set on doing what I want to do, and I assert that no one, even God, has a right to tell me otherwise, then this seems like a harsh restriction. But I want to suggest, this may be an unwarranted impugning of the character of God for at least two reasons:

1. The slave was in the unfortunate position he was in by choice – both making bad choices and choosing to survive by bonding himself for six years to a master. Marrying was probably never a wise choice during that bondage period, as until he was free again the jury was out as to whether he had learned to support himself, let alone a wife and children. Still, hormones are hard to fight, especially without

[36] Jonathan B. Krasner, Jonathan D. Sarna, *The History of the Jewish People: Ancient Israel to 1880s America* (Milburn, NJ: Behrman House, 2006), 1.

strong opposing incentives to act appropriately. For evidence just consider the number of "baby daddies" who indiscriminately father children they never support or care for in a meaningful way.

2. The wife and children of a man who was unprepared to be either a husband or a father are not just better off, but probably saved from certain death in the harsh conditions of the ancient world when left in the protection of the owner. This restriction, like every seemingly harsh restriction placed by God, I propose, is for the better flourishing of the innocent parties in this transaction.

It is simply unrealistic, short-sighted, and ignorant to apply modern standards and sensibilities to the ancient world, just as much as it is to apply them to our world of just a hundred (or so) years ago. Then and now, God is always taking people where they are, accepting them that way, but not leaving them there. He leads us into more equitable and free relationships not only with one another but more importantly with Him.

Contrary to skeptical opinions, it is not God we see growing from one Testament to the next, but His people. God created people with tremendous capacity to grow as moral creatures, both toward morality and away from it. Within 1500 years the practice of slavery was dramatically different, and the Scriptural advice given by Paul in the book of Philemon, regarding the escaped slave Onesimus, was to receive him back as a brother in the Lord.

Another way non-Christians may be short-sighted on this issue is because of their preoccupation with justice in this world, something God is not nearly as interested in. That preoccupation makes sense if this is the only world, but it also means there will never be any justice, as no matter how hard we work for it, justice will never characterize every person's life and existence in this world.

God's preoccupation in this world appears to be two-fold: Restoring people to His family and conforming them to His image. While all of us prefer to avoid harsh environments and challenging circumstances, these conditions are often used as God's means of accomplishing both purposes in us.

I am keenly aware that I have not answered this objection exhaustively. For all thinking and compassionate people these are important issues. I have not even touched on the enslavement of captured battle enemies. There is much to cover since we are talking about the lives of such a distantly removed culture. For a more comprehensive treatment I point you to the excellent book by Paul Copan, *Is God a Moral Monster?* which is listed in the Bibliography section of this volume.

Your God Endorses Slavery

1. Compare your present feelings to a character in *The Wizard of Oz*. Which character are you (tonight) and why?

2. Start by sharing. Are there people in the group for whom some Old Testament passages have been challenging? Did they find any help as they read this week's chapter? How so, or why not?

3. Imagine the flow of a conversation with a skeptic who brings up this topic: What questions might you ask to help them fairly consider the topic?

4. The "fallen world" defense is a cohesive part of the Christian worldview. It states that many things about the world are not as God desires, or would have intended, but that a brokenness of the world system(s) was/is a necessary consequence of granting us free will. What do you think about that?

5. What, if anything, should the author have addressed, that you feel he "left on the table?"

Pray for one another to be fearless and bold in Kingdom work. Voice your feared inadequacies with one another and pray specifically that God will help each one in your group to become a better witness – more apt, more ready, more willing, and more fearless.

Chapter Eight

Science is All That Matters

Science and scientific discovery have done much to bless the world, from vaccines, and medicines, to computers and rockets. It is easy to see, therefore, especially when someone lacks a belief in God, how they could conclude that science is all that matters. But that idea is almost embarrassingly easy to refute. You must be careful not to embarrass those who believe it, to preserve their dignity, and not just send them running with their tail between their legs. Science is far from "all that matters" even to the people who say it is.

Okay, the statement is rarely made exactly like I have stated it, but the sentiment, or the "gist" of the statement is a recurring atheist refrain. "I'm not religious. I am a woman of science," might be their triumphal statement, indicating the supposed incompatibility. They will often add that "Christians are 'anti-science,' or even 'science deniers,' so we accept 'magic and fairy tales' that no rational person could believe." For good measure, they often throw in a warped and a-historical take on Galileo's house arrest, as if his science put him so at odds with the church that he was cast, bound in chains, into a dark dungeon. None of that is true, but in some ways, short of reading books I recommend in the Bibliography, you will just have to take my word for it, as I do not have the space to refute it in this volume.

People who insist that "your religion" denies science will start with that assertion, but it's often not their end game. Eventually, they demand that you provide "scientific proof" for the existence of God. "I won't believe anything that cannot be proven by science." Unfortunately, they are (often) dismissing God because He is too large, too omnipresent, too ubiquitous, and magnificent to reduce to their methodology.

The irony here is that just by making such a statement they are demonstrating how little they know about the limits of science. "Proof" is not generally available through the scientific method, so science neither "proves," nor "disproves" anything, especially (perhaps) the existence of God. Philosophers of science are aware of this, and in near uniform agreement about it.

Persons who assume the incompatibility of belief with the disciplines of science often insist that Christians are at odds with science, or uncomfortable with scientific ways of reasoning, drawing inferences, making careful observations, and presenting conclusions. The record suggests that the impression is mistaken and misguided.

It is well-known that the roots of early scientific thought, at least in the Western world, were dominated by (self-identified) Christians. Faith skeptics usually attribute this reality to the fact that in those periods of history the world was awash in superstition and ignorance and there was an unfair dominance of the church over most aspects of life, even the practice of the sciences, which were known, at the time, as "natural philosophy." "Now that we've stepped out of the Middle Ages," so the reasoning goes, "we should jettison our old superstitions and embrace science for our answers." There is, undoubtedly, some truth in that observation, but it fails to deal with a larger point; that such a world fostered the seeds of thought that led to the development of modern scientific methodologies. Without question, such modalities were developed to study more earnestly the wonders and the handiwork of God.

Many people believe that the situation among today's working scientists is dramatically different and that one would be hard-pressed to find Christians doing any serious work. Two prominent sociologists, Elaine Howard Ecklund and Robert A. Thompson, Jr., wrote an article in a recent edition of Christianity Today, wherein they summarized findings from their book, *Secularity and Science: What Scientists Around the World Really Think About Religion*. According to their careful studies, while the picture of contemporary Christians working in fields of science is ever-evolving, the primary evolution seems to be toward more, not less of such involvement. Presently, "we found that nearly a quarter of our US scientists identified as Christian."[37] That's a strong percentage, especially considering the amount of publicity the supposed conflict between science and faith is given. There is no way of knowing the number of Christians who have steered clear of careers

---

[37] Elaine Howard Ecklund and Robert A. Thompson, Jr., March, 2020 (Boone, IA: *Christianity Today*), 52.

in science due to the supposed conflict between the two. Christians who are also scientists have found reasons they find compelling and sufficient to warrant their involvement. More importantly, when interviewed, working scientists (overall) see no conflict between their science and their faith.

The percentage of Christians is even higher when one considers the highest performing scientists, those who earn the distinction of winning Nobel Laureate status for their work, as more than 60% of Nobel Laureates in various scientific categories, are Christians.[38] Why should this be, especially considering the perceived conflict? Several factors may be at play; including the same motivations that spurred on early Christian scientists and the sense of "calling" which often accompanies such work today, especially in the fields of medicine and ecology. In the Christianity Today summary, "One biologist told us, 'My religion pushes me towards research of medical value because helping other people is important to me.'"[39]

People who think belief in God is a limiter on doing good science have never made a persuasive case for that opinion. Moreover, as it turns out, the idea that science is all-encompassing and should, therefore, be all-consuming, is also patently false. Science is quite limited in the answers it can provide. They are often very important answers and Christians love finding them, but it is quite silly to think they are the only worthwhile answers.

---

[38] John C. Lennox, *Can Science Explain Everything?* (Charlotte, NC: The Good Book Co., 2019), 17.
[39] *Christianity Today*, March, 2020, 53.

Dr. William Lane Craig, the brilliant philosopher, theologian, and Christian apologist, participated in a discussion following his debate with Oxford Chemist, Peter Atkins, in which Atkins asserted that anything truly worth knowing was knowable through the scientific method. He went so far as to claim that science was "omnipotent," which is as close as you will likely find to someone admitting that the practice of science is their god. Craig, obviously pleased, sat up in his chair and responded by listing five things, off the top of his head, which science cannot explain: logical and mathematical truths—these must be "presupposed in order to do science," metaphysical truths like the existence of other minds and the external world, ethical values, aesthetic judgments, and most importantly, the scientific method which Atkins asserted was "omnipotent."[40] At that point the moderator, the late great William F. Buckley, stepped briefly outside his neutral role and told Atkins to "Put that in your pipe and smoke it."

What is going on in the minds of many who make statements such as Peter Atkins made amounts to a kind of worship of science, called scientism. Such people are persuaded by the notion that science is all that truly matters and that it will eventually provide all the answers that really matter as well. While far from true, this philosophy has caught the ears of several atheists and agnostics. Such persons see themselves as pure, unadulterated empiricists, holding only to what can be scientifically supported, evaluated, and verified. Concomitant with that

---

[40] https://www.youtube.com/watch?v=BQL2YDY_LiM retrieved 10/22/2024

is (often) the belief it is their noble duty to dispel the delusions of "science deniers," i.e., those who refuse to agree with their philosophical position.

But is it a "denial" of science to recognize that, as a discipline, it is limited in what it can hope to explain and accomplish? Is it a denial of science to propose theories that observe the same facts and evidence but make proposals that differ from the mainstream consensus? Of course not, especially when those theories make better sense of the facts and data.

Let us consider an analogy: Am I denying the efficacy of a baseball glove if I refuse to acknowledge its effective use as an airplane? Hardly. It is a wonderful tool for catching baseballs, but it is not, in any sense an airplane.

Is it even conceivably possible that scientism is a logical and coherent worldview? No. It is just another atheist "swing and a miss," a "silly thing," not carefully thought out, and certainly not sensible. So, my advice is to reframe Dr. Craig's impromptu list as polite questions: "Wouldn't you consider logical and mathematical truths to be of at least *some* importance? Those must be presupposed *to do* science, but we don't know about them *from* science, at least we didn't initially." "Wouldn't metaphysical truths like the existence of other minds and the external world, ethical values, and aesthetic judgments be of at least *moderate* importance? If so, how do you maintain that science is all that matters?"

Finally, if God is largely inaccessible through the scientific method, though much of science plausibly infers His existence, then arguably the most important Thing of all cannot be discerned through science, making science a far cry from "all that matters." This statement, of course, is viciously circular. But it is no more fallacious than the statement, "Science is all that matters," especially when uttered by people who primarily say it while disagreeing with any scientific inferences that point to God. Many atheists are only making such a statement because they think it further separates them from anything to do with Him. They are quite mistaken.

Here is something I use when someone asserts this opinion, "If Science and Christianity are at such odds, why are over 60% of Nobel Prize winners in science categories Christians?"[41] Sometimes a knowledgeable skeptic will respond that "93% of the members of the National Academy of Sciences are atheists." I never quibble about their statistics. That figure is widely published, so it may be correct. I also am not trying to be confrontational. Remember, questions are almost always better than statements. Here is what I often say when these two statistics are on the table. "Well, that is quite a discrepancy. I know my figures are accurate. What do you think accounts for it?"

When I give someone the respect of valuing their opinion in a non-confrontational way, more often than you would think, they will become less strident, and more conciliatory, and the whole tone of the conversation will lighten up. My goal is to get to a place where we are having a conversation, not a battle. I want them to become open to the possibility that I may be right, or at least that not everything

---

[41] John Lennox, *Can Science Explain Everything?* (Charlotte, NC: The Good Book Co., 2019), 17.

they believe is necessarily 100% correct. But to get there, questions, respect, and gentleness are the order of the day.

Truthfully, there are several areas that many Christians may disagree with most scientists, especially about biological evolution. There are also quite a few working scientists who have expressed reservations or outright rejection of that theory. It is not usually productive to discuss evolution, however you feel about it, except in generalities and then only when your skeptical friend asks.

When someone asks me about it, I have a stock response you may find useful. "There are Christians who believe in evolution. In fact, they probably represent *most* Christians. Now, admittedly to believe that way they must view the book of Genesis differently than I do. Whatever you think about that issue, the thing that makes someone a Christian is *not* their view on evolution, but their acceptance of the Lord Jesus. And Christians are not unlike scientists. We don't walk in lockstep on every issue. God made us all unique and we don't check our brains at the door when we receive Christ as Lord. Are you familiar with the "Dissent from Evolution" list? You can read all about it in *The New American* magazine, even the online edition. It is a large and growing list, currently over 1,000 PhD-level scientists, who do not believe evolution is true.[42] I think they're right, but I'm not a scientist."

In summary, science matters. It is not all that matters. It is far from all that matters. As a Christian, I see science as the most effective way

---

[42] https://thenewamerican.com/over-1-000-scientists-openly-dissent-from-evolution-theory/ retrieved 10/24/2022.

to study God's natural world, something that has helped us make major discoveries, important breakthroughs, and enormous progress. I am not at odds with science and Christianity as a whole, is certainly not either. Scientism expects more and asks more of science than it can provide. People who use their love of science as a smokescreen to avoid God are stepping out on a broken limb and should be disabused of the false notion that Christianity and God are disproven by science.

Science is all That Matters

1. On a scale of 1 – 10, how are you doing at this point in our study? Are you learning new things? If so, what? Are you being encouraged and strengthened? If so, how?

2. Were you surprised that such a high percentage of Nobel Laureate scientists are Christians? What, if anything, do you conclude from that fact?

3. What do you think of "scientism?" Had you heard or read about this term before? How might some knowledge of what is wrong with scientism help you share Christ with people who believe Christianity is anti-science?

4. Do you have strong feelings about the supposed divide between Christianity and science? Do you have useful ways of dialoguing with skeptics who feel they must choose between the two? What do you say?

5. How do you feel about the author's response to the question of creation vs. evolution? Do you have a different response that you prefer? If so, what?

Close in prayer. Pray for insight and wisdom for your group members, as they share Christ. Pray for any specific concerns and needs in your group.

Chapter Nine

I Can Be Good Without God

This one is hard to explain. In one sense it is entirely true. Someone who does not know God can (in theory) comply, at least externally, with behavioral norms and expectations. It is also highly probable that at least *some* people who have a true relationship with God are capable of immoral behaviors that would make the average sailor blush, and I mean no disrespect to sailors. To our shame, many who know Christ are just as likely to be involved in public and private sins and there may be many atheists who surpass the morals of those Christians.

But there are at least two ways they are not truly being "good without God." First, God grounds what is good to begin with so, while they may seem good by comparison with other humans, no one is truly good, but God alone. I can be reckoned (an accounting term) as good, but only by having a right relationship with God. And second, denying God is never "good."

There is a syllogistic argument for the existence of God which is strongly related to both points. It has two premises and a conclusion.

1. If objective moral values and duties exist, then God exists.

2. Objective moral values and duties exist.

3. Therefore, God exists.

While there are various versions of this argument, called "The Moral Argument," this one is probably the simplest form.

Syllogistic arguments, like this one, are either valid or invalid. Arguments are most plausibly true if both premises are more plausibly true than not, and if the conclusion follows from the premises. But, for atheists, the conclusion, "therefore God exists" is a particularly hard one. It points in the direction that our sinful nature does not want to be true and wishes was not. So, the atheist response is normally to deny one or more of the premises,

The moral argument begins with the fact that all normal people, those without a psychological defect, recognize that moral values and duties do exist. These are values to which we subscribe even if we do not live up to them. Some things are right, and some things are wrong. Even when we are choosing to do the wrong thing, we know that thing is wrong. We make excuses to ourselves and even plan what we might say if we are caught, but we are not under the illusion that just because we want to do something—that very fact, somehow makes it okay. We have a moral conscience.

If we did feel we are a "law unto ourselves," that whatever we choose to do and however we choose to live is right, even in clear violation of our conscience—our inner moral compass, that would be a definition of subjective moral values. But, intuitively, without even being told, almost all people know better. Moral values and duties *must* be objective as people cannot hope to live peacefully with others if overarching values are not shared. Society cannot endure each person being a law unto themselves.

For proof, we only need to put the shoe on the other foot. I may be able to live with the fact I cheated on someone, for example, but it's wrong for you to cheat on me. I might be able to justify a longer than approved lunch break, or even fudging my timecard as an employee, but I do not want you doing those things if I am your employer. Most people, throughout the world, even crooks, liars, and charlatans, know where the broad moral lines are drawn.

But *why* do we all know this? When we demand to be treated fairly or complain something is not "right," we are appealing to a standard above ourselves, an objective standard to which we assume everyone is aware, and with which everyone agrees. Moreover, we assume that standard cannot be arbitrarily changed. Otherwise, you may not like what I do, but you have no right to expect me to behave according to your personal whims. When any behavior is wrong for all people, everywhere, and always it is therefore (necessarily) rooted outside of humanity. The only alternative is that all our shared moral intuitions are wrong and morality itself is illusory.

All moral laws, obligations, and duties, especially those that transcend individual whims, that are true regardless of what we want to do and how we feel about them, require a lawgiver. If we are the arbiters, even corporately—the "societal we," then morality is subjective and no one has a right to hold anyone accountable for any behavior, regardless of how abusive, aberrant, rude, thoughtless, callous, heinous, or twisted.

But we all know, even every atheist, that rape is never okay, juggling babies in the air is immoral, and any number of things, not because we are personally offended by them but because they are objectively wrong—wrong for everyone, no matter what, where or when. Moral values are so intrinsic that even toddlers try to be sneaky and surreptitious when doing something wrong.

If such laws are objective—true for all people, everywhere, always—then the lawgiver *transcends* us. The only plausible candidate to hold such a position is Someone Who transcends humanity— Someone we call God. Those are the reasons premise one is fairly airtight, although many atheists will argue for the illogical idea that morals arose from evolution, which is often referred to as "survival of the fittest."

But survival of the fittest should not favor honesty, altruism, and truth-telling – it should favor pragmatism. If our morality arises from our evolution, it does so in opposition to the supposed evolutionary mechanism. We can certainly see how looking out for yourself, and a winner-take-all mentality, running rough-shod over those who get in our way favors individual survival, but how does evolution, even moral evolution lead to altruistic, even selfless behaviors, acts of heroism, and the acceptance of personal risk for the benefit of others? These important features of morality are indicative that it neither arises from evolution nor is it of natural origin. The fact that we all agree that the latter is preferred to the former is further proof that morals are objective.

The second premise in the argument, therefore, is practically superfluous, for once the first premise is acknowledged, the conclusion that God exists inexorably follows. But so what? What does His existence have to do with me? For one thing, if He exists then all other beings, including me, are contingent. We owe Him for our very existence. That is a reality that is suppressed every time we behave immorally, whether in secret or in the open.

That is the point of my second observation: Denying God is never good. Suppression of the conviction of the Holy Spirit, whether I am living an otherwise moral life, is a stubborn, obstinate, and rebellious way to respond to the Giver of life, and is therefore by definition, immoral. Such rebellion is arguably the most immoral act because it has its roots in the original sin of pride. Whether someone can be "good without God," is not nearly as important a question as "Why would someone want to reject, dismiss, and rebel against the One Who died so they could have everlasting life?"

Now, certainly, if they are suppressing the truth, and do not believe there are reasons to believe in God, then they do not see that they are making such an error. I believe many atheists are not seeing the evidence for God because they are actively suppressing and ignoring it for moral reasons. They do not want to have anything to do with anyone, even God, telling them how to live or behave.

It is amazing how many men and women go through a "faith crisis" while cheating on a spouse or becoming involved in some other moral dilemma. Humans are not wired to live with such inconsistencies. It is hard for us to actively live in ways that are contrary to our consciences, so in our determination to continue to write our own rules and be our own bosses, we sear and seek to eradicate the conscience that condemns us.

I do not subscribe to the idea that people motivated in that way are in any true sense "good persons." Moreover, on the Christian worldview, no one is a "good person." "All have sinned and fall short of the glory of God." (Romans 3:23). When I protest that I am a good person, or that I can be good without God, I am proving I do not understand His standard—perfection, which was only achieved by the Lord Jesus. Unless His sacrifice is appropriated on my behalf I am lost and without hope in this world and in the world to come.

Now, convincing an atheist to drop their definition of "good" to replace it with the biblical definition is probably a big ask, but it's a worthwhile goal – something to shoot for as the conversations continue and the relationship strengthens. It is what evangelist Ray Comfort is doing when he regularly asks people, "Do you think you're a good person?" The answer to that question is almost always, "Yes," because most people are comparing themselves with other people, rather than the standard of righteousness, God Himself, expressed perfectly in the Lord Jesus.

Every person who truly becomes a Christ follower must make the step of acknowledging their sinfulness – of seeing themselves in need of saving, therefore needing the Savior. Any protest of how good they can be without God, or how they do not need God to live a good life is a sad example of how desperately they need Him. The objective, when conversing with someone who believes this silly slogan, is not to claim some personal moral superiority over them, but to point out the universal need everyone has for the Savior, "for all have sinned and fall short of the glory of God" (Romans 3:23).

You're no better. Without Christ, we are all in the same fallen condition, blood guilty, and must pay for our sin. Even people who loudly protest that they do not believe in God or accept the reality of their condition, are still in the same unenviable fallen condition, and God will still Judge them for the law they broke. Many people are in prison, throughout the world, for breaking laws they felt were unfair, or capricious, or of which they were completely unaware. Ignorance of the law does not even work as a defense in this life, and it will certainly fail at the final judgment.

The whole subject of morality is messy and somewhat imprecise, mostly because of the human predilection to self-justify. The psychological and emotional tension of living in a consistently immoral state, constantly failing, over and over, by doing things you know you shouldn't do, is a condition that leads one to either deny their actions are immoral, or to crave cosmic forgiveness and redemption. There are many concrete examples.

I have read and heard dozens of testimonies from women who tried very hard to be convinced and to convince themselves that it was okay to terminate their pregnancy on the abortionist's table. The details vary, but the broad outlines of their testimonies are remarkably similar. They tried in vain to bury their guilt, sometimes for decades, but the harsh reality of what they had done continued to haunt them until they found true freedom and forgiveness in Christ.

There are many stories of abortion providers who were living with the same inner burden. Intuitively they knew what they were doing was murder, but the pay was good, or they felt they were fighting for reproductive rights, and they performed all sorts of mental gymnastics to justify themselves to themselves. After all, you may not have to live with me, but the one person I cannot escape is myself. We cannot live well in constant states of moral dissonance.

Comparable stories abound in the community of those who formerly practiced all kinds of sins, even if society supports and affirms their failings. Remarkably, even when someone is unable to fully forsake the immoral behavior, they are still more emotionally stable, better adjusted, and more at peace when they take the step of acknowledging and admitting to their sin, rather than continuing to justify it and defend it. Over a period, with the Lord's help, they can even overcome, or severely lessen the frequency of their moral violations – simply by taking the step of admitting what their heart already knows, that the act(s) they desire to commit are immoral.

The Bible calls this acceptance, "confession." The original word comes from combining two words which mean "same word." To confess sin is to say and believe the same thing God does about my sin, i.e., that it is sinful and wrong. Repentance starts with this change of heart. That change appears to be the single most important element for a change in direction and changed outcomes. Most people are aware that the first step in addiction recovery is to admit the addiction, to claim it as one's identity. For the time being, society supports addiction recovery for drugs, over-eating, and alcohol, or at least there are no alcohol pride parades. Do not be surprised if that changes, because while morality itself is objective, the human tendency to justify immorality is extremely strong.

Human weaknesses, what the Bible sometimes calls "besetting sin," and the recovery community calls "addictions," are stubborn and difficult to eradicate – demanding a lifelong, sustained effort. But they are impossible to attack without first admitting they exist. Serial offenders often waste decades, or even a lifetime, belligerently refusing to acknowledge, and deeply burying the painful truths that are eating away at them. These psychic fractures cannot be buried so deeply that they do not cause all manner of depression, anxiety, and other emotional unrest, because morality is objective. We do not get to pick and choose like ordering at a moral smorgasbord, and at some level, everyone knows that.

Before you get judgmental—perhaps your moral failing was not used as an example—remember you are no better off than anyone else. Your condition, without Christ, is deplorable. Atheists who awaken to the reality of objective morality should hope there is restoration and forgiveness in Christ, or at least somewhere, as the alternative is a lifetime of frustration and anxiety. In my experience, such hope is often a first step to finding Him, and the peace He brings through repentance and faith.

We should offer a question when confronted with the slogan that people can be good without God. "Then tell me, in your opinion, why aren't they?" It is a simple response but make sure you have time to sit and talk because this "silly thing" is often getting to the root of the problem many atheists have with God, and such conversations require a thoughtful, respectful, and well-considered approach.

Be careful about your demeanor. Being a jerk towards anyone, especially someone you are seeking to win, is not only immoral, but also plain dumb. You do not know anyone, nor will you ever make the acquaintance of someone you can look down on from a lofty, elevated position of moral superiority. Your immorality may be the current soup de jour, you may hide it well, or God may be helping you forsake it, but it is no less wrong. Christ is the universal equalizer. The most effective preacher, the evangelist, and the small group leader all need Him just as desperately as the drug dealer, practicing homosexual, or prostitute.

But it is also vitally important not to equivocate. When asked, "Is this or that sin?" answer truthfully but kindly. "Yes, it is, and He is in the sin-forgiving business." Or "Yes, the Bible says all of us are sinners, and Jesus came to save us." God does call us to live in ways that are opposed to our inner tendencies.

We tend to devise a lie rather than risk embarrassment. We tend toward self and have never actually loved any neighbor or thought as often or as highly of a neighbor as we do ourselves. We sin as a default position and must learn to yield to God. No one must teach us how to cheat, steal, lie, or roll our eyeballs at a parent. Even though our conscience condemns us, we choose disobedience because it seems more expedient.

The moral argument for the existence of God is particularly good for making a beeline to the cross. People cannot help but think of their own moral failures when confronted with the objective reality of morality itself. So, make sure you are ready with good seed to sow in the fertile soil of a heart God may be awakening to truth. This course is only a part of your equipping process. That process is something you should joyously pursue for the rest of your life, or until He returns.

Never forget how it felt to be lost, . . . and to be found. Keep asking leading questions. When you lead me to discover the truth, rather than beating me over the head with it, the only person I can argue with is myself. In the appendices of this volume, this author provides several good questions, as well as conversation starters, and other helpful materials. Familiarize yourself with them. Make them a part of your witnessing arsenal.

Sometimes, especially when presenting a syllogistic argument, it is easy to get off into the weeds, arguing minute and petty details. Some atheists with whom you speak will have studied these arguments more than you have, poking holes, and looking for weaknesses. It is in their interest to deny the force or weight of the conclusions. Here is a simple phrase I like to remember. It is from a Keith Green song. "Just keep doing your best. Pray that it's blessed. He'll take care of the rest."[43] It is not your decision. You have already made yours. Keep living in the reality, truth, force, and power of that decision. Live by faith in the Son of God.

---

[43] Keith Green, "He'll Take Care of The Rest" Sparrow Records, 1977

I Can Be Good Without God

1. Test yourselves. Can people in your group remember the exact wording of the "moral argument for God?"

2. Briefly discuss defenses for each premise.

3. Discuss the connection between the moral argument and forgiveness in Christ. What are some ways you might steer a discussion of the argument in that direction?

4. Is there anything that stood out to you in this week's study?

5. Is there anything about which you disagreed?

Share burdens, praises, concerns, and needs with one another and pray for one another.

Chapter Ten

Even Christians Are Atheists

Yes, you read that right. This clever statement, and variations of it, has been a staple of the atheist's arsenal for at least a few decades. The idea is explicated as follows: "You are an atheist concerning millions of gods, from Thor to Zeus, to the millions of gods in the Hindu pantheon. I simply go one step (or one god) further and also dismiss yours." They often continue, "I dismiss your God for the same reasons you do not believe in Thor or Zeus."

Something sounds wrong with those statements, but you might be having trouble putting your finger on it. The problem is one of apples and oranges. There is no meaningful comparison between Jehovah God and Thor, or Zeus. They are not analogous. Your atheist interlocutor might as well be saying, "I dismiss the notion of horses because there are no unicorns," or, "I dismiss all money because there is such a thing as counterfeit money." Those are non-sequiturs.

Are Christians atheists? Technically, . . . no. Atheists deny the existence of God and gods, or, at the very least, are unconvinced of the existence of any god. Christians are not only convinced there is a

God, but we also go a step further and believe we know Him, walk with Him, and hear from Him. If we are of obviously sound mental fitness, living productive, creative lives, that fact alone should cause pause for those who find it easy to dismiss us.

So, the first part of the statement is a non-starter, an obviously "silly thing," if they believe it. But that is not the genius part anyway. That is just the "attention grabber." That is what they say to catch your attention and pique your interest. The crux of the statement is in the last part: "I dismiss your God for the same reasons you do not believe in Thor or Zeus."

Ouch! That sort of lands. That seems strong. If that is true it is not at all silly. It would mean God has left Himself indistinguishable from legions of false gods. It would mean there is nothing, or not enough, uniquely special about our experience of God, or our intimacy with God, and nothing substantively exceptional and/or different that sets Christianity apart from false religions. More to the atheist's point, it would mean our God is no more real than all the false gods.

Face it; if all that is true, even without the ultimate blow, they have still made a strong point, one of their strongest. The underlying contention is that people make up gods all the time and ours is made up too. More on this later, but it may be of some importance that atheists are tacitly admitting that people are made for worship. How else does one explain man's tendency, in all cultures, always to develop concepts of god and constructs for the worship of gods and goddesses?

The general assumption of atheists, of course, is there is nothing special about *any* religion—nothing that sets it apart or makes it worthy of consideration more than any other. Tantamount with that assumption, walking hand in hand with it, is the underlying thought that all religions are mere human contrivances. All religions, at least in that sense, are alike. That is a running theme with many hard atheists. Your testimony is not unique to Christianity. Your ethereal/transcendent feelings and experiences are nothing special and can be explained by brain chemistry. You are a Christian because you worship man-made notions about a man-made god— nothing more.

So, I love it when someone says it to me, despite how formidable the declaration appears to be. There are three, and possibly four vulnerabilities to the statement, and to the overall sentiment it conveys. I usually do not carpet-bomb all of them in a single encounter. None of them, by the way, are a slam dunk, or undefeatable rebuttal. I do not think they have to be, because the atheist's assertion is not based on anything more than their opinion about my psychological state. And it is their assertion that should be placed on the defensive. If they are going to make an assertion, they should be required to have a warrant for it. As C. S. Lewis wrote, "If you are a Christian, you do not have to believe that all the other religions are simply wrong all through. If you are an atheist, you do have to believe that the main point in all the religions of the whole world is simply one huge mistake."[44] First, Christianity seems to

---

[44] C.S. Lewis, *Mere Christianity* (New York, NY: HarperOne, 1952, 2001) 35.

be nothing (remotely) like anything its earliest adherents would have made up, which goes against the notion that they did (make it up). Start with Jesus being both God and man, an idea that is inescapable from even a cursory reading of the New Testament. Jews are famously monotheistic and therefore had no easy way to reconcile this fact about Jesus, either internally, with how they already believed, or externally, with their culture. The violent opposition and life-threatening reaction from their society would also seem to mitigate against early Christians simply making it up. Most people do not intentionally fabricate lies that could obviously and easily result in their own demise.

Second, one purpose of this statement, and/or often arising from it, is the idea that Christianity is pretty much like every other religion. All religious people have the same "experiences" but label them differently, depending on which god/religion they attribute them to. Christians are delusional when they think there is anything special about their own ethereal experiences. All ecstatic experiences are better attributed to human psychological states than to actual supernatural encounters.

Your spiritual experience of Christ is the same as a Mormon "burning in the bosom," a Hindu's "trance," or a Muslim whirling dervishes' ecstatic state. All religions have identical experiences because they are all within the realm of, and induced by chemicals in the human brain, not actual encounters with a higher spiritual plane. Further, since such states are admittedly subjective, you have no way of *proving* your spiritual encounters are not substantially the same as people who reject most or all the doctrines you embrace.

What should also be obvious here, is that the atheist making such a statement also has no way of comparing one spiritual state to another. What he is offering, like the experiences he is critiquing, is wholly subjective. He may be right. He may be wrong. One conclusion would seem no more certain than the other. Bald assertions need not be responded to since they offer nothing objectively testable. One could easily respond to this assertion by asking, "Why do you think so?" That is what I did for years, and it may still be a good way to tease out a more thoughtful conversation.

Let me stop and just admit, this objection had me stymied for a few years. I knew that my awareness of Christ was real, but I had no way to demonstrate it was substantially different from the Mormon who *knows* her own experience is similarly *"real."* One day, while meditating on this objection, an answer occurred to me. It seemed at once so obvious I was not sure how I had missed it, and so simple I was sure it could not be *that* easy.

I was thinking of the first ex-Mormons I had spent considerable time with. Early in my ministry, I met the most wonderful couple, Mike and Michele Hobbs. I was a youth pastor and they had recently begun attending our church and bringing their two teenage kids with them. Their kids, Mickey (a girl) and Billy (a boy) were sure of what they believed, mature in their faith, and committed to Christ, in no uncertain terms. As young parents, my wife and I wanted kids that grew up to love the Lord and we were open to sound advice everywhere we could get it.

Meeting Mike and Michele was life-changing and Christ-affirming. We quickly became fast friends, and no one who knew the Hobbs, even for a short length of time, went long without hearing their testimonies of finding Christ and leaving Mormonism. They had both made the journey to Christ together. When they met and married, Mike's lineage was Mormon and Michele was a lapsed Catholic. Mike had been LDS (Latter Day Saints) for several generations. It dawned on me, thinking about our friends, that the charge that Christianity is just like every other religion was one they would find completely ludicrous.

Mike and Michele were now fully committed to Christ, and the difference, in their estimation, was like night and day. The contrast could not have been starker. If it *was* the same, they could have just remained in Mormonism. Admittedly, we are still dealing with their subjective feelings, but I contend that people in a position to *know*, not just *assert* that all ethereal experiences are identical, to a person, would likely testify that they are *not*. And the beauty of this insight is that practically all conversions, from one worldview to another, mitigate against the claim. It does not even matter which way the conversion goes, whether into or out of Christianity. There has likely never been a convert who testified, "I realized my ethereal feelings of encountering God were completely the same—there was no discernible difference, so I flipped a coin and decided which one to base my life on."

On the contrary, there is almost always a dramatic difference, a Mike and Michele Hobbs difference—a conversion. We "convert" from one religion to another, often through great soul searching, tears, and emotional angst. To cheapen that experience by simply asserting that all religions are the same is profoundly tone-deaf.

Neither side can *know* whether another person's subjective, experiential *encounter* with Christ is real, at least not with complete and utter certainty. But surely the benefit of the doubt in such an argument should go to the people testifying of their personal encounters, not the side holding their fingers in their ears chanting, "liar, liar pants on fire."

Before leaving this point, a word of caution is in order: Many atheists are people who think of themselves as "former Christians," which is highly unlikely, but rarely worthwhile arguing about. They will accuse you of the "no true Scotsman" fallacy, and neither side can easily prove their point. The "no true Scotsman" fallacy of logic is a form of equivocation, and it also begs the question. It is essentially employed by asserting that someone's behaviors are not, by subjective measure, indicative of the position(s) they claim to hold or to have held. Therefore, they are mistaken about belonging to the group or ever belonging to the group with which they claim the prior affiliation. "Proving" your point requires a rather sophisticated theological explanation about which even the church is in some disagreement.

While we may have good theological grounds to assume "once a Christian always a Christian," so anyone claiming they were *formerly* Christian is mistaken, these are not the kinds of arguments that lend themselves to anything less than a fully orbed discussion. Most of the time you have a large enough task explaining how/why other gods are not analogous to God. There is rarely a need to deny the personal experience(s) of your interlocutor, needlessly adding another layer of tedious discourse.

Third, there are far too many cases of radical and dramatic life-changing conversions that created lasting transformation for generations, for there to be, in the words of Gertrude Stein, "no there there." Not only are Christians not atheists, but you would be hard-pressed to find a Christian who does not know another Christian for whom becoming a Christian saved their life. These radically changed lives are too numerous *not* to be noteworthy, and unrivalled by commitment to secular humanism, atheism, or any other anti-god worldview. And the exceptions, those persons caught red-handed in horrible hypocrisy, are also noteworthy because they are in such stark contrast to an overwhelming pattern to the contrary.

For a God Who does not exist, He is awfully potent. He is certainly busy, quite involved, and active, with a powerful ability to do what no number of drugs or therapies seem able to accomplish, and a track record that far exceeds what other individuals can do, even the ones atheists acknowledge exist. Atheists, of course, offer alternative explanations and other causes for the effects that seem undeniable.

I am not offering subjective conversions as proof of an objective God, but when the only thing atheists offer is their own subjective opinion that my experience is invalid and add to their speculative conjecture that my experience of God is materially no different from those of any and every other religion, I cannot only answer in kind but also refute them with overwhelming testimony to the contrary.

I stated that there are possibly four vulnerabilities to the mindset that sees God as a man-made invention. The fourth "answer" is not necessarily available to everyone. That answer, for me, has to do with some unique, non-normative, very special times when God has clearly spoken to me, given me knowledge I could not empirically possess, or performed some miracle, healing, or other proof which would serve to convince any rational person that He exists. These do not happen predictably, nor every day, but in over four decades of serving Him they have happened enough that, try as I may, I can think of nothing that more rationally explains these events than that God is real, He cares, He is all-powerful, and sometimes He materially and obviously intervenes.

All this is not to claim any sort of special status with God. I have been more fortunate than many of His followers to view some dramatic miracles, but it is not because I am more holy. In some cases, it may be, however, that I am more apt to pray and ask Him to intervene. "You have not because you ask not."

Here is the substance of an answer to the assertion "I dismiss your

God for the same reasons you do not believe in Thor or Zeus." First, I agree with them. Yes, you read that correctly. *They* probably *do* reject God for the same reasons *they* reject Thor and Zeus. But I shouldn't. I do not have a personal relationship with Thor or Zeus. I have not vetted any historical, philosophical, or testimonial evidence for the existence of Thor or Zeus. And, while such an investigation might be stimulating, it would not likely produce any information that caused me to conclude differently about Christianity.

Why? The God I *have* vetted has indicated that He is the *only* true and living God, and He does not lie. If He is Who He says He is, and the evidence suggests that He is, then all other gods are pretenders, perhaps of human invention, maybe Satanic imposters, or based on misunderstood natural occurrences, but they are not Jehovah God. It truly is a matter of apples and oranges, perhaps even apples and airplanes—as there is a vast difference between God and the millions of man-made gods, or spirit pretenders.

There is a connected argument with which you must be acquainted—an additional verbal jab that often accompanies this idea. Atheists will say, "You only believe in your God because of where you were born. If you were born in the Middle East, you would be a Muslim, in India, you would be a Hindu, and if you were born in Finland, or Switzerland you might even be an atheist, like me. Whatever faith you profess you learned from your parents."

Even though such logic commits a form of the genetic fallacy,[45] it

---

[45] The "genetic fallacy" is an informal fallacy that attempts to dismiss the truth or falsity of a proposition because of how it came to be known.

is still more likely to be true than not. But even so, it is irrelevant to the truth claims and evidence for Christianity. The same kind of thing could be said of someone living deep in the heart of the African continent or the Amazon, as a person in an undiscovered tribe. One could say, "The only reason you do not believe in X, Y, or Z is because you are ignorant of it." While that assertion may certainly be true, the genetic origin of what one believes has nothing to do with *whether* the belief they hold is accurate. If X, Y, or Z is true, it is true regardless of how it came to be known. It would even be true if no one knew it.

Further, your atheist friend is often a living, breathing counterexample of what she is claiming. Say, for example, she was born in America. By her "logic," she would be a Christian since that is the majority religion in America. People leave the religions they were born into every day. Behind this assertion is a rather severe misconception about God, one the church has not always been helpful to correct.

The assumption that God would act unjustly, as an unrighteous Judge, condemning people based solely on their lack of a sufficient gospel witness, is Scripturally unwarranted. Unfortunately, there are many Christians who have given this subject short shrift, and they are not armed with the ways the Bible addresses the subject of those who have either not heard, or whose knowledge of Christ is severely flawed or restricted. In common parlance, this is referred to as "the issue of those who have never heard."

We should not be too obstinate to admit if people are damned to hell merely by "accident of birth," or largely because of *where* they were born, then an indictment of God's character logically follows. Is His offer of salvation largely limited to those fortunate enough to be born in the right places? Does God "so love" only certain parts of the world, so that "whosoever" is born in a predominantly Christian nation may have the opportunity to receive Christ and not perish?

Unfortunately, the "answers" that are often provided, even from some otherwise sound Christian sources, are often less than helpful. These explanations do little to rehabilitate an aberrant view of God's character. Many of the answers are based (almost entirely) on a strained interpretation of some passages from Paul's letter to the Roman church.

Everyone, wherever they live, whatever they have heard or not heard, has non-specific (so-called) *general* revelation of God. Nature, combined with common sense, and our spiritual feelings of awe and wonder, are enough to convince any person of sound mind that God exists, He is holy, and we are not. That much seems evident.

But a common interpretation of the operative passages suggests that *no* one, having such revelation, responds in a way that pleases God, so he condemns every person without clear and direct knowledge of Christ. He shows no mercy. If that is the case, we are left with the impression that God, Who knows everything, has *still* left some people with no *actual* way to be saved. Apparently, God has provided enough general revelation to condemn, but not enough to excuse or to save.

But, in Romans 1:20-32, what if Paul was teaching about what happens to those who respond *poorly* and he was *not* indicating, one way or another, what happens to those who respond *properly* to the light they are given? There is nothing in Paul's text that precludes the possibility that God will 1) provide more knowledge of Himself to those who are responding appropriately, or that he will not even 2) save (outright) people (through the blood of Christ) who do not know the *name* of Christ or possess more specific revelation. That latter point is the more controversial position, but Jesus appears to lend it some support.

The oft debated and controversial view that there will be some saved *through* the blood of Jesus who, nevertheless, lack specific revelation about Him is known as inclusivism. Growing numbers of evangelical scholars seem to be leaning toward or accepting inclusivism as true. As Millard Erickson explains, "The rise of more inclusive views of salvation, even among evangelicals, is based on a belief in the efficacy of general revelation for a salvific relationship to God."[46] He continues in the same vein:

> What if someone were to throw himself . . . upon the mercy of God, not knowing on what basis that mercy was provided? Would not such a person in a sense be in the same situation as the Old Testament believers? The doctrine of Christ and his atoning work had not been fully revealed to these people. Yet they knew there was provision for the forgiveness

---

[46] Millard J. Erickson, *Christian Theology* (Grand Rapids, MI: Baker Academic, 2013), 123.

of their sins, and that they could not be accepted on the merits of any works of their own. They had the form of the gospel without its full content. And they were saved.[47]

While those who oppose the inclusivist view are concerned that it makes the sacrifice of the Lord unnecessary, Erickson strongly disagrees,

The basis of acceptance would be the work of Jesus Christ, even though the person involved is not conscious that this is how provision has been made for his salvation.
. . . Salvation has always been appropriated by faith. . .. Nothing has been changed in that respect.[48]

As I implied earlier, this view (inclusivism) may have direct support from the Lord Jesus, as recorded in John 15. Our Lord talked with His disciples about how the *world* (Christ rejectors) would treat them poorly because of their association with Him. For those scanning the Scriptures for an answer to God's disposition toward those who have never heard, or those who have arguably had an insufficient gospel witness, something (often overlooked in that passage) provides a ray of hope. About such people, Jesus plainly says, "If I had not come and spoken to them, they would not have sin; but now they have no excuse for their sin." (vs. 22). Further down, in verse 24, the Lord states it slightly differently, "If I had not done among them the works which no one else did, they would not have

---

[47] Millard Erickson, *Christian Theology*, 138.
[48] Ibid., 138.

sin; but now they have both seen and hated Me and My Father as well." It at least seems like if there are people Christ has not spoken to, or to whom He has not proven Himself, in ways He deems sufficient, they will *not* be condemned by the sin on their record. At least that is how grammar works and is how inclusivists see it.

From the position of defending the faith, it is not important whether the growing number of theological inclusivists are correct, but only that there are numerous biblically conservative, orthodox ways of thinking about the issue of people who have never heard the gospel. It is frankly silly for an atheist to think they are privy to some insider secret that upsets the whole Christian apple cart. Christians have been studying, meditating on, and thinking seriously about our doctrine for two millennia, and we have not been awaiting the arrival of an armchair atheist theologian to discover that we had never bothered to consider whether those doctrines cohere.

I prefer to remain agnostic on inclusivism and I do not think God saw fit to tell us exactly how He will deal with this issue, but from everything we know about Him, we can trust He has it well in hand. He will do the right thing. He is both just and merciful. If He was looking for ways to condemn, He would not have sent the Son in the first place.

No, Christians are not atheists, and Christianity is unlike the religions with which it is compared—far more dissimilar than similar. The trajectory of this line of thought is flawed from the outset, so the permutations that follow are also at odds with the truth. Although your atheist friend has a difficult time seeing it, the Christian worldview is

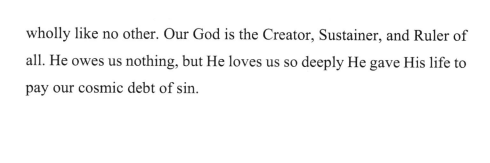

wholly like no other. Our God is the Creator, Sustainer, and Ruler of all. He owes us nothing, but He loves us so deeply He gave His life to pay our cosmic debt of sin.

Even Christians are Atheists

1.   Talk about why you chose this class and subject: Are you happy with what you are learning? Why, or why not?

2.   Imagine being in a conversation and having this week's "silly thing" verbally thrown at you. What are some ways you would respond? Would you feel obligated to respond at all? Why, or why not?

3.   What do you think about the issue/problem of those who have never heard? Have you ever thought much about this topic?

4.   Is there anything that stood out to you in this week's study?

5.   Is there anything in this week's lesson about which you disagreed? What? Why?

Share burdens, praises, concerns, and needs with one another and pray for one another.

Chapter Eleven

Religion is a Mental Illness

Once the person with whom you are speaking stoops so low as to insist that your beliefs indicate you are mentally ill, it may be a good idea to retreat for some length of time, perhaps a few days, before re-engaging them in more constructive dialogue. This rhetorical charge is usually thrown out in disgust or anger, so you might have been asking for it. If you owe an apology, make it quickly and sincerely. Be the bigger person. We represent the One who looked out at those who called for and carried out His excruciating execution and said, "Father, forgive them, for they do not know what they are doing." The person saying, "religion is a mental illness" probably is not so stupid as to believe it. But strictly speaking, it is still a silly thing, and even sillier if they *do* believe it.

This "silly thing" is a popular meme, T-shirt, and bumper sticker slogan, and a favorite charge to hurl at Christians who are getting on the nerves of overly sensitive atheists. It is so absurd it is hard to imagine it as much more than that, but when you look further into it you discover that several prominent atheists have been suggesting it may be true, as far back as Sigmund Freud, and its history probably did not begin with him.

> [Freud] was plainly obsessed with religion, treating it repeatedly in such books as "Totem and Taboo" (1913), "The Future of an Illusion" (1927), "Civilization and Its Discontents" (1930) and "Moses and Monotheism" (1938), comparing the "wishful illusions" of religion to "blissful hallucinatory confusion," religious teachings to "neurotic relics," and religion itself to "a universal obsessive compulsive neurosis" and "a childhood neurosis."[49]

As a loud and notable opponent of all religions, Freud had few equals in his time. But today many of the most popular atheist figures have echoed his refrain, jumping on a swelling bandwagon that seeks to reduce and diminish religion by dismissing those who practice it as being mentally defective. Writing in his book, *The Selfish Gene*, Richard Dawkins declared that faith itself "seems to me to qualify as a kind of mental illness."[50] Philosopher Sam Harris concurs. Writing in his bestseller, *The End of Faith*, "It is difficult to imagine a set of beliefs more suggestive of mental illness than those that lie at the

---

[49] https://www.deseret.com/2017/2/2/20605291/is-religious-faith-a-mental- illness retrieved 10/29/2022
[50] Richard Dawkins, *The Selfish Gene* (New York: Oxford University Press, 1989), 198.

heart of many of our religious traditions."[51]

Freud, Dawkins, Harris, et al, were/are likely not altruistically concerned with the emotional and mental well-being of believers, as much as they desire to position themselves, and those of their ilk, as the height of mental normalcy, juxtaposed against psychologically *inferior* believers. From their perspective, it is easy to see why they feel like they do. We believe in a worldview and propositions they strongly oppose, and we are doing so without a shred of evidence. In their opinion, we even believe despite strong evidence that our views are wrong. We are, in other words, strongly delusional.

Roughly defined, a delusion is a firm, fixed, false belief that is not moved or altered by reason or evidence. Ironically, I feel, by that definition, that many atheists are delusional, especially a few I have been praying for and speaking with for some time. They have been exposed to philosophical, historical, and scientific arguments, personal testimonies, miracle data and documentation, etc., of the same kind that God uses to move other people to receive the Lord Jesus and place their trust in Him. Yet they continue to resist, deny, and reject Him. Why?

One reason is that atheists, like humans in general, have cognitive dissonance. All of us tend to seek out ways the world and our circumstances can match what we *want* to be true—for there to be, in other words, a harmony between the way things are and the way we would like for them to be. When two or more modes of thought are

---

[51] Sam Harris, *The End of Faith: Religion, Terror, and the Future of Reason* (New York, London: W. W. Norton and Company, 2004), 72.

contradictory, we often choose the one that coincides with what we *wish* to be true. Neural science refers to the mental discomfort we experience, while trying to reconcile the contradictions, as cognitive dissonance. For example, I have a hard time, although I try to witness to atheists regularly, articulating all the various shades, nuances, and objections they use to justify their lack of belief in God. One reason for that is that their objections fall outside of my worldview, the way I think the world works, so my brain pushes them to the periphery of my thinking, not to be considered in my day-to-day decisions.

There is also likely another neural factor at play. Like you and me, atheists are good at practicing confirmation bias. Confirmation bias is the practice of giving more weight and value to data and information that tends to confirm my opinions, and considerably less value to any information which would challenge or oppose them. The atheists in your life, and those you meet and witness to, are likely no more or less likely than you are to have at least part of their thinking clouded by confirmation bias.

Thankfully, the evidence for God and the evidence for the truth of Christianity is not only stubborn and strong but is mixed with the conviction of the Holy Spirit, conviction of a type that works its way not only into our mental processes, but our souls. People who leave their worldview to accept Christ and the Christian worldview, are often surprised that God's love was able to break through their mental fog and bring the clarity they needed.

When I hear that my Christianity is a form of mental illness I am tempted to respond, "Thank God. Don't get me any treatment. I've never been more content, happy, and free." I don't, but I am tempted Instead, I start by asking questions. "What do you mean by that?" "How did you come to that conclusion?" "What neurotic, unbalanced, or odd behaviors do I have?"

Mental health is a serious issue, and many people suffer from poor mental health. Christians are not immune to that suffering. Whichever way you respond to the slogan that Christianity/Religion is a mental illness, avoid the temptation to make light of it and turn it around on your atheist rival. People suffering from mental health issues come in all sizes, shapes, and varieties, and it should be an issue that is so serious it should not be co-opted to be used in service to a pejorative comment about any group of people.

The only way to meaningfully talk about "a group" of people, in the aggregate, is to have a large enough sample, over a significant period, to yield data demonstrating whether supposed correlations are caused by their identity with the group. That is true of any group. Several researchers have studied the mental health of religious people, including Harold Koenig of Duke University and Tyler Vanderweele of Harvard, both of whom claim that religious people appear to be significantly more mentally and emotionally fit than the general population and (especially) the non-religious. No less of an authority than the Mayo Clinic found that religious people and the "spiritually observant" enjoy physical and mental health and a resultant better quality of life than the non-observant.[52]

But the statement "religion is a mental disorder" is not about any of that. It is not about the actual psychological state of believers. It is just another way of saying what has already been said, much of which we have considered in previous chapters. Atheists, not content that they have stated their opinion strongly enough when asserting (without bothering to rebut evidence) that there is "no evidence for God," become desperate enough to marshal the spectre of mental illness in their quest to dismiss Him. If you are mentally ill, I do not have to deal with your arguments. When someone is resorting to this demeaning tactic it may constitute evidence that your formidable arguments are landing. They are getting through so soundly that I must dismiss the message by dismissing the messenger.

So, even if Christianity results (overall) in more well-adjusted, stable, content, purpose-driven, happy individuals—at least as a group—it is *believing* what Christians *believe* that leads atheists to characterize them as ill. Christians are ill by virtue of those beliefs, even if all other evidence points to their remarkable mental soundness. How is one supposed to counter such a content-free criticism? Should we even bother?

At the risk of boring you by repeating myself, the statement of the late Christopher Hitchens comes back to mind, "What can be asserted

---

[52] Mueller, Dr. Paul S. et al. (December 2001). "Religious involvement, spirituality, and medicine: implications for clinical practice". *Mayo Clinic Proceedings vol. 76:12*, pp. 1225-1235. Retrieved from Mayo Clinic Proceedings website on July 20, 2014.

without evidence can be dismissed without evidence."[53] If your questions fail to move the conversation along in a positive direction it might be time to quit again, at least for a time. Leave the conversation open, if possible, and keep praying.

I regret this is so, but in hundreds of conversations with atheists, they have often shown themselves to be petty, irritated, on edge, and agitated. Sometimes they see it and even admit that they behaved poorly. I even had one tell me, referring to a previous conversation we had, "It's pure irony that I acted so crazy," his words, not mine.

I try to be the bigger person. I was too stunned to think well on my feet. I wish I had replied, "I don't think you are crazy. I believe you think you have reasonable, rational, and logical reasons for believing what you believe. I think you're wrong, but I don't think you're crazy. It seems like we might make more progress if neither of us thinks we're dialoguing with someone so irrational we might as well not bother." I do not always say the right things on the spot.

When someone resorts to name-calling, impugning your intelligence, calling you crazy, or mentally ill, the enemy of your soul wants to gin you up into an irrational, mean-spirited, visceral response. Because of the potent combination of cognitive dissonance and confirmation bias, no matter how many logical points you have scored, once you lose your cool that will likely be the only thing about the conversation they vividly remember. Remember, their brain is

---

[53] Christopher Hitchens, *God Is Not Great: How Religion Poisons Everything* (New York, NY: Twelve Books, 2007), 150.

looking for ways to dismiss you and your arguments for God, and if they cannot find any legitimate reasons, they will use whatever passes for one—including how "crazy" you are. "I can't believe this guy! All I did was tell him he's a lying, mentally ill, stupid person and he went nuts. I knew Christians were crazy, but this guy takes the cake."

Sometimes it is tough to keep your cool and avoid being offended, but atheists are prone to make statements like this one to keep from dealing with your arguments. Dismissing you is easier than dismissing what you are demonstrating. Don't give up on them that easily. Atheists need champions who will befriend them anyway, love them anyway, believe for the best in them, and trust for the scales to fall from their eyes. They need you.

On a final note, on this subject, please do all of Christendom a favor and do not be crazy. I am not talking here about mental illness, but the crazy way some Christians are hyper-critical, unloving, dismissive, judgmental, and/or unkind. Jesus is so winsome, and His personality is so attractive that, when He was on earth, people would shinny up trees just to get a glimpse of Him. They would hang on His every word to the point of refusing to leave His presence even when He spoke far into their mealtime.

If you are trying to speak *about* Him or *for* Him without spending time *with* Him, and without being enthralled by Him—to the point of becoming like He is—true discipleship, then repent and fall back (figuratively) at His feet. If you would rather talk sports than spirituality, repent. If you prefer acceptance, reputation, income, or your way to His way, repent. Why would you want to lead someone to accept Someone you barely acknowledge? Following Jesus means I live my life depending on every word that comes from His mouth, growing to become like Him, to have His priorities, and His compassion for the lost, broken, despondent, and hurting.

Be hard *not* to like. The longer someone is forced to reason and consider alternatives to their worldview, the harder it is to continue entertaining confirmation bias. Do things with your atheist friend just because you enjoy their company. Go bowling. Play cards. Do life together. You don't need to be constantly hounding them about God. Keep it obvious where you stand. Say things like, "I better be headin' home. I get to gather with the church in the morning." You can only say and do so much, and the rest is between your friend and the Holy Spirit.

Interestingly, the same author (Peter) who wrote the verse most often quoted by apologists, 1 Peter 3:15, about always being ready to defend why you believe, had written to wives with unbelieving husbands, just a few verses earlier. He wrote, "You wives, be subject to your own husbands so that even if any of them are disobedient to the word, they may be won over without a word by the behavior of their wives, as they observe your pure and respectful behavior." (1 Peter 3:1- 2).

Like the wives Peter was writing to and about, once you have strongly made your bold stand for God with a skeptical friend you do not necessarily need to make every subsequent encounter a time for debate. You have made it clear why you are the way you are, and why you do what you do. When you let them off the hook, by not pressing the subject in every subsequent meeting, the Holy Spirit continues to speak, draw, and convict, accomplishing inner work you could never do. During those times, while you're not speaking directly to your friend about God you should never stop talking to God about your friend. You should also continue to walk in probity and live righteously.

Occasionally, as you continue living an overcoming, victorious life, you can find special reasons to invite your friend to somewhere the gospel will be presented. Will your child be singing in a Christmas show at church? Is there a special game night with your small group? Is there a Christian movie you can go see together? "Look, I know this isn't your kind of thing, but I'd love to take you to BBQ and see this movie together." Sometimes, as the Spirit is moving and working on them, people say "yes," and some people eventually say "yes" to the meeting which becomes the occasion for their surrender to Christ.

The Apostle Paul plainly stated what stance you should maintain. "But as for you, brethren, do not grow weary of doing good" (2 Thessalonians 3:13). Similarly, the writer of Hebrews encouraged his readers to follow the example of Jesus and to "not grow weary and lose heart" (Hebrews 12:3b). Your mindful and careful Christian walk is as important, maybe more so, than having all the answers or responding to every complaint. Live like someone aware of the axiom, "actions speak louder than words."

Religion is a Mental Illness

1. Do a checkup. How are you? What has you wondering? Worried? Wounded? Witnessing?

2. Imagine being in a conversation and being told, in so many words, "You only believe that because you are mentally ill." What do you say, or how do you respond?

3. Is there anything from this week's study that grabbed your attention? What? Why?

4. Did you disagree with the author about anything in this week's study? What? Why?

5. What gives you pause about stepping out to share Christ with those who consider themselves atheists?

Share burdens, praises, concerns, and needs with one another and pray for one another.

Chapter Twelve

Jesus Was/Is an Imitation and a Myth

A view known as "Jesus Mythicism" is held by a small minority of scholars and a great many atheists. Nowhere in their theories do they satisfactorily explain why people would conspire together to concoct a myth that would make them social outcasts, and how, despite fierce and militant opposition they would stick to their stories, enduring persecution, and rejection with, so far as we can tell, not a single defection. Those are uncomfortable nuisances that just get in the way of a blind, unsupported, irrational assertion that the earliest Christians simply made up the Jesus character. A variation on that theme is that the person (Jesus) was real, but His exploits and biography were/are mainly fictional.

One of the most enduring recent examples of someone supporting this theory is Gerald Massey, a 19th-century English poet and amateur Egyptologist. His ideas are so attractive to some atheists, especially non-scholarly types, that despite being fully and widely discredited they are widely disseminated and often cited in popular media and literature. Mr. Massey wrote an essay, *Historical Jesus, Mythical Christ*, the thesis of which was/is that the unique, distinct, authenticating features of Jesus' biography were lifted (stolen) from Egyptian mythology. Bill Maher, an American atheist, comedian, and social commentator featured Massey's theory, in some detail, in his movie, *Religulous*, as did an internet film, *Zeitgeist*, which seems to be attracting an inordinate amount of attention.

Proponents of this form of mythicism propose that some past myths have the same characteristics of the Jesus story: virgin born, the gathering of 12 disciples, teaching followers, commanding nature, casting out demons, betrayal by a friend, dying, and rising again, birth attended by three wise men, born on December 25th, . . . the list expands and contracts, depending on who's telling it. Those who wrote about Jesus took parts and pieces of existing myths and reworked them into one of their own. They were wilful deceivers, and we are blind and gullible followers.

If they were deceivers, if we are gullible followers, and if Jesus' story is a retelling of earlier myths, they have a valid point. They were not; we are not; and it is not, so they don't. Still, because many atheists believe Jesus is a pasting together and re-contextualizing of ancient myths, such as Horus, Mithras, and Osiris, they question why we consider Him to be unique. The question often posed is why we think the stories of Osiris, and other mythical saviors are fictional, but treat the same stories as factual when referring to Jesus?

I must admit, when I first heard of these alleged similarities, I was thrown for a bit of a loop. I wasn't sure what the answer was. Sure, some of the things were easy to rebut, such as the December 25th date and the "three wise men," since those are not actually part of the Bible narrative to begin with. If we borrowed the date, and the number of people bringing three kinds of gifts (gold, frankincense, and myrrh) I was fine with that—it didn't jeopardize biblical Christianity, just some later additions never a part of the inspired text.

I also reasoned, upon further reflection, that ancient myths never had living, real historical figures through which their stories could be corroborated. They were purely mythical, with no tangible ties to ancient people who could (even remotely) testify to seeing, let alone knowing, touching, and interacting with any of these so-called gods. The history of Christ and His followers is qualitatively different.

Take Polycarp, for example: Living from AD 69 – 155, he was the Bishop of Smyrna and a disciple of the Apostle John, who learned first-hand about Christ from the writer of four New Testament documents. He wrote a letter to the Philippians that gives scholars significant information as to how well-regarded the New Testament was in the church, quoting from it several times in his short epistle. Polycarp's disciple, Irenaeus regarded the memory of Polycarp as a tangible connection to the apostolic past. Irenaeus relates his Christian testimony in a letter he wrote to Florinus, another student of Polycarp:

> I could tell you the place where the blessed Polycarp sat to preach the Word of God. It is yet present to my mind with what gravity he everywhere came in and went out; what was the sanctity of his deportment, the majesty of his countenance; and what were his holy

exhortations to the people. I seem to hear him now relate how he conversed with John and many others who had seen Jesus Christ, the words he had heard from their mouths.[54]

This kind of historical connectedness is found everywhere in the earliest history of Christ and Christianity and nothing anywhere close to such historical confirmation may be found for *any* of the mythical gods. But maybe, as time progressed, people prone to make up stories, whatever their motives, just got better at it, possibly even conspiring together to become first-hand "witnesses" to the alleged Person they were chronicling. Certainly, if I am intent on following truth, the similarities between earlier myths and Jesus deserved investigation. Besides that, I have no interest in pursuing a cleverly devised tale, no matter how comforting.

Christianity stands apart from every other religion with which I am familiar in that, at least in theory, it is falsifiable. If we found the verified bones of Jesus, or we uncovered true, first century autographs (documents written in the subject's own hand) wherein the Apostles confessed to the Jesus hoax, then Christianity is not true. This "copycat" theory is dangerously close to the latter.

When people are contemplating God, and/or if people have encountered Him, a certain amount of similarity would seem natural. Those similarities, such as the deity being able to control nature, heal sickness, and do other miracles is not necessarily noteworthy and

---

[54] Fr. Paolo O. Pirlo, SHMI "St. Polycarp". *My First Book of Saints*. Sons of Holy Mary Immaculate – (Parañaque City, Philippines: Quality Catholic Publications, 1997), 58–59.

certainly doesn't indicate copying. If the proposed deity could *not* do those things they would not qualify, in any sense, for the title "god." A royal title and heritage, ritual meals, being foretold by a prophet, possessing supernatural power, even being portrayed as a shepherd— none of that is surprising. As Jim Wallace points out, "If divine beings protect and guide humans, we might expect the ancients to associate them with shepherds."[55] Shepherding was a common profession and would have therefore been a common analogy.

But setting aside those kinds of unremarkable similarities I still had the issue of some features that were not so easily explained. When I looked closely, however, the theory started to unravel. For one thing, as it turns out, the "similarities" between Jesus and the mythic prototypes were always greatly exaggerated, and often, it seems, entirely invented. From (at least) Massey forward, mythicist authors have been freely quoting one another, but rarely quoting original sources, and *never* about *any* of the most novel and interesting claims.

When there are slight similarities, those instances are enormously magnified and greatly exaggerated. They are superficial similarities that mythicists almost always add to outright deceptions, half-truths, and untruths to try to make a literal mountain from even less than a mole hill. Take, for example, the oft-cited "resurrection" of Osiris. Entirely unlike Christ, he was not truly resurrected at all, but simply awakened in the underworld.[56] To call such an event a resurrection is

[55] J. Warner Wallace, *Person of Interest: Why Jesus Still Matters in a World That Rejects the Bible* (Grand Rapids, MI: Zondervan Reflective, 2021), 33.
[56] Craig S. Keener, *The Historical Jesus of the Gospels* (Grand Rapids, MI: Wm. B. Eerdmans, 2009), *336.*

a total misrepresentation.

I was unable to corroborate, from any of the earliest, most reliable sources, similarities to which an unbiased observer could point to as copied from ancient myth. Instead, I found several assertions that can most charitably be characterized as "undocumented," therefore scholastically sloppy, and at worst as fraudulent. If the authors had historical sources for the claims of similarity which they were making, then they failed to provide them, preferring rather (apparently) to quote one another, and providing no historical chain connecting their assertions with documentation outside of their echo chambers of doubt and denial.

An example of one of the ways parallels are not truly analogous is Mithras and his alleged "virgin" birth. The claim is that Mithras was born of a virgin and that's a parallel with Jesus, but not even the mythical Mithras was born of a virgin. Mithras was born out of a rock, which is unusual but hardly parallel. If the mythicists just pointed out that Mithras had an *unusual* birth, which is true, it would undermine their fallacious case, so, quite often, they simply change the story to strengthen the impact. In other words, they lie.

A major popularizer of some of the most egregious claims is American comedian and political commentator Bill Mahr. Consider these words from Bill Maher's 2008 movie, *Religulous*:

> Written in 1280 BC, the Book of the Dead describes a God, Horus. Horus is the son of the god Osiris, born to a virgin mother. He was baptized in a river by Anup the Baptizer who was later beheaded. Like Jesus, Horus was tempted

while alone in the desert, healed the sick, the blind, cast out demons, and walked on water. He raised Asar from the dead. 'Asar' translates to 'Lazarus.' Oh, yeah, he also had twelve disciples. Yes, Horus was crucified first, and after three days, two women announced Horus, the savior of humanity, had been resurrected.[57]

You would think, in a big-budget movie, released throughout the world, that producers would diligently research such an audacious claim, so it *must* be true. Arguably, not a single word in the above paragraph can be supported by neutral, unbiased scholarship.

Space does not permit a one-by-one refutation, but I will tackle a couple of the claims. Let's start with the "virgin birth" of Horus. Maher has zero scholarly support for his claim. There is not a single source for the myth of Horus in which he was born of a virgin. His mother, Isis, is not a virgin when she gives birth to him. There is nothing in the earliest extant sources about any virgin birth of Horus, and the most complete telling of his birth narrative, which still does not even hint of a virgin birth, was written by the Greek historian and Middle Platonist philosopher Ploutarchos of Chaironeia, who lived c. 46 – c. 120 AD.

Okay, so he missed on that one, but you must admit the story of Anup the Baptizer is suspiciously close to the story of John the Baptist, especially since they were both beheaded. It would be if there was a shred of support for it. Maher's claim that Horus was baptized by "Anup the Baptizer" is just as bogus as his virgin birth assertion. First, there exists no figure by the name of "Anup the Baptizer" in ancient

---

[57] *Religulous,* (2008), Thousand Words Productions, dist. by Lion's Gate Entertainment.

Egyptian mythology. The name Anup is most likely a transliteration of the name of the Egyptian god Anubis, but Anubis was not remotely associated with *any* form of baptism. Worse still, for Maher's theory, Anubis was never beheaded.

I tried, I really did, but alas in vain, searching throughout the scholarly record to support even one of Maher's alleged parallels to Jesus, but each claim failed as spectacularly as the two I have outlined. Either Maher thought no one would fact-check him, or he failed to fact-check wherever he accessed his material—either way it's complete hokum. Whether Maher made them up, or more likely, accepted them uncritically and without vetting them, the claims are wholly untrue. They make for interesting copy—a compelling script, fit for Hollywood, but unfit for scholarship.

A second issue with the "scholarship" of mythicists has to do with some matters of their interpretation of the few documents they use. I found instances where they accepted that a reference to an earlier god was unaltered and trustworthy even though the only records of that deity post-date the New Testament era. Why, unless you have a theory in search of support, would you assume Christianity borrowed from a source documented *after* its inception, rather than the other way around? Common sense would indicate that older religions might borrow from the new kid on the block (Christianity), since it was growing in popularity and notoriety, especially when earlier documents included no such similarities. The previously mentioned birth account of Horus, written by Ploutarchos of Chaironeia, who lived c. 46 – c. 120 AD, is a prime example.

Quite a few honest scholars of antiquity have pointed out that the parallels asserted by Maher and others are spurious, and comparisons which seem closer to the mark (though still wildly different) are probably of more recent vintage. If anything, the powerful impact of Christianity led followers of other religions to retell their own stories, so they more closely resembled the gospel accounts. As the formidable Bruce Metzger noted,

> The larger issue is the question of who influenced whom. With Christianity exploding onto the scene of the Roman Empire, it is evident that other religions adopted certain teachings and practices from Christianity in order to stem the tide of departing adherents or, perhaps, to attract Christians to their side.[58]

When you scratch below the surface you find this seemingly impressive objection evaporates. The venerable Tryggve N. D. Mettinger, retired professor of Hebrew Bible, at Lund University, Sweden, described the case, "There is now what amounts to a scholarly consensus against the appropriateness of the concept [of dying and rising gods]. Those who still think differently are looked upon as residual members of an almost extinct species."[59]

One of the biggest problems with asserting an alleged influence of pagan mythology on the formation of Christianity is that Jews, who

---

[58] Bruce M. Metzger, "Mystery Religions and Early Christianity," in *Historical and Literary Studies* (Leiden, Netherlands: E.J. Brill, 1968), 11.
[59] Tryggve N. D. Mettinger, *The Riddle of Resurrection: "Dying and Rising Gods" in the Ancient Near East* (London: Coronet, 2001), 7, 40-41.

comprised many of Christ's first followers, would have been the *last* people in the first-century Roman empire who were likely to embrace a god who shared pagan attributes.[60] Jews were strict monotheists, and living where and when they did they were likely to know the stories about pagan deities and would have roundly rejected all efforts to tie in their true and living God with those myths and stories.

Even in non-Christian, Jewish writings, I could find no record of rejecting Christ because He was/is a retelling of pagan myth. Such an idea could not have arisen while the myths were well-known, and people were still worshipping many of the gods in question, precisely because the Christ figure was unlike those gods wholly and completely. He is singular and unique—the One with Whom other religions compare, copy, and the One they often try to castigate.

Since He cannot logically be ignored, thinking people must try to impugn Him in some way. If I cannot dismiss Him, it is reasonable to assume I must deal with Him. His name becomes a curse word. His churches are blamed for everything wrong with the world. His messengers must also be dismissed as half-baked kooks and/or charlatans, for the alternative response, yielding to Him, humbling myself, and pleading for His mercy, forgiveness, and grace, to many (perhaps most) skeptics, is horrifying and unthinkable.

Jesus mythicism is a bit touchy to talk about because a lot of people who espouse it do not know, from a scholarly perspective, how propositions should be defended. If you have read this far in this book

---

[60] J. Warner Wallace, *Person of Interest,* 35.

you know the art, practice, and science of historiography is quite involved and requires careful, deliberate, thoughtful work. Most atheists you will meet, and virtually all the atheists who support the notion of Jesus Mythicism, especially those who believe Jesus was a copy of pre-existing pagan myths, have not bothered to make a thorough investigation. They assume people like Bill Maher can be trusted, mostly because they agree with his conclusions. Any conclusion that helps someone continue to suppress the truth of Christ is just what they've been looking for, so they accept it uncritically. They may further assume that whatever support they can find in published form is also trustworthy. It has probably never entered their mind that the sources they are quoting may be utterly mistaken on the facts.

Remember, as often as possible, to use questions. Here is a good one for this topic. "I have investigated this a bit, and I don't think it has scholastic merit, but I may have missed something. Would you be willing to provide me with any written documentation, dating from *before* the time of Christ, proving the most serious claims you are making?" Please watch your tone—stay gentle and respectful. Stay friendly, kind, truly curious, and engaged. If you're looking to quickly rebut a position someone is heavily invested in, so you can knock it aside and get "preachy," that's not likely to go well.

I have been having these conversations for over four decades. I have noticed, so long as I am fair, that most people will give me something approaching equal time. Practically no one, however, is interested in being preached to, letting me dominate our conversation, or in having me shame them for their ignorance. When you are friendly and fun to talk with, the Holy Spirit can use you to minister Christ to a surprising number of people.

I suspect one of the things that most frustrates skeptics is that Christianity is still having a powerful and noticeable impact on the modern world. It is so forceful that many of them are willing to believe almost anything to keep from believing Christ. The idea that Jesus was simply the latest in a long line of mythical dying and rising gods will do as good as any, so long as you don't investigate it too closely. But the subject on the table should be the same one Jesus asked His disciples, "Who do you say that I am?" (Luke 9, Matthew 16, Mark 8).

Whatever answer someone has, it is not a question educated people should take lightly. In his book, *Person of Interest,* J. Warner Wallace convincingly develops the thesis that Jesus is, by far, the most consequential person Who has ever lived, in all cultures, for the past two thousand (plus) years. That is reason enough that informed, responsible, educated people should study His life and determine where the evidence points. To swallow lies we agree with is just as bad as rejecting truths with which we disagree. Your atheist friend deserves to learn the truth about Jesus, so they can make a fully informed decision about whether they will love, follow, serve, and worship the One Who died for them.

Jesus Was/Is an Imitation and a Myth

1. Ask everyone in the group to give a quick report on how they're doing this week, spiritually, emotionally, and physically.

2. What are your thoughts about this week's topic?

3. Have you faced this kind of criticism of Christianity before? What did you think about Jesus being reduced to comparisons with pagan deities?

4. Rate your level of confidence (from 1 – 10) when dealing with this atheist belief. Why did you rate yourself the way you did?

5. Do you have any favorite parts of this chapter you would like to discuss further?

Pray for the mental, spiritual, and physical needs of those in your sphere of influence. Ask God to give you genuine, caring friendships based on mutual love and respect, with people who are far from Him.

Chapter Thirteen

Churches Do More Harm Than Good

Here we are at the final (for now) silly thing atheists believe. Unfortunately, the list of silly things is so long that I may not have covered, in this volume, one you have heard or read. Some which I *have* covered may strike you as rather odd choices. I had to be selective, but I am not "ducking" anything. Everything I have ever read or heard, from atheists attempting to deny or impugn the reality of God, can be meaningfully rebutted with a bit of research and some thoughtful consideration. After decades of interacting with atheists I am confident they have no ultimate defeaters to Christianity and no good reasons to reject the voluminous evidence refuting their positions.

I hope you are learning to look beyond, and in addition to, specific arguments, and you are seeing how to think *about*, and look *behind* the issues that atheists raise. Essentially, atheists' beliefs and statements about God fall into three categories:

1. <u>Slogans</u>—Bald, unsupported assertions. As mere assertions, they do not technically require a response. It is even an unsupported

assertion to say that your experience of God is a delusion, since I cannot empirically know someone's subjective experiences.

2. Complaints—Rants against the character or nature of the God they do not believe in, often aggravated by their errant take on Scripture, and/or their desire to not be restrained or contained by God's moral boundaries. The defeater for this position is a revelation of their own unworthiness, and His mercy/grace.

3. Ignorance—They do not believe in a god, or in some facet of Christianity, because of their straw man caricatures, or gaps in their knowledge. They often do not like me saying so, but I do not believe in the god many atheists are rejecting. That one does not exist.

It is frequently helpful to discern which of the categories you are dealing with, as you discuss and analyze specific statements. A slogan, for example, can sometimes be easily disarmed by simply asking, "What makes you think so?" At the very least, the answer to that question may help you formulate a productive conversational framework.

When someone's primary statement boils down to a complaint, I have found it helpful to bring some clarity by asking, "How does that matter to you if there is no god?" Or, even, "I disagree with your interpretation of that, but suppose you are right, how does that prove there is not a god?" Complaints are either from poor hermeneutics, or a sinful desire to disallow God His sovereign rule. The latter is a category error, arising from a confused understanding, that would allow someone to suppose God must answer to His creatures rather than God's creatures answering to Him.

Even if I thought there *was* no god, I hope I would be wise enough to realize that, if there *was* one, I would not oversee him, he would oversee me. This rather elementary logic seems to elude many atheists, ironically constituting some of what demonstrates their spiritual blindness and bankrupt worldview. The reverse, man telling God what to do, in any rational configuration of the world, simply does not follow.

Sometimes an atheist's belief is not easy to pigeonhole or cannot be contained by only one category. Such is the case, for example, with the oft-held opinion that churches are doing some sort of horrendous social, emotional, and mental damage to the world. It may even be said to be a general atheist's consensus, especially among the unsophisticated and not too scholarly types, that churches do more harm than good, an idea that somewhat fits in all three categories.

People who believe the church is genuinely harmful are often the kind who are not troubled enough to learn the details and who avoid the risk of allowing good data to get in the way of bad arguments. They are rarely aware, for example, that the arts, (visual, architectural, musical) were sustained and maintained by the church as their primary benefactor throughout large swaths of human history. They are similarly unaware that the church gave rise to the scientific method they often revere, the higher education they seek to dominate and control, humanitarian efforts such as hospitals and hunger relief, the anti-slavery efforts in the Western world, and social reforms that brought dignity and equality to all classes of people.

If the spiritual mission of the church also has merit, then all that humanitarian progress is icing on the cake. It is *that* mission, the spiritual one, that frustrates and disturbs atheists the most. Yet it can only be successfully argued that the spiritual mission is a blight or burden if it can be established that the transcendent mission of the church is not true. Some academic atheists are an exception, but the average atheist does not even try to establish a positive case against God and against the truth claims of Christianity.

Atheists insist that we (Christians) are making positive assertions that we cannot know. To *know* we are wrong, however, the atheist would have to *know,* not simply contend we are wrong, which they do not. That is why the statement, "Churches do more harm than good," qualifies as a silly thing atheists believe. Since the humanitarian effort is largely unrivalled and unequalled, one would have to prove there is psychological damage that overrides it, creating a net human deficit. The rubric demonstrating that deficit would also need to be justified.

Typical of much of their complaining, this grievance is not entirely groundless, or at least one may see where the seeds of such an attitude have been helped to develop. The church, Christ's body on earth, is far from perfect in either worshipping or representing Him. It is full of people who are flawed, finite, and sinful—right down to every member. But so is every institution led by people since all people are similarly flawed.

Christians are forgiven, and the best Christians desire to live in grateful obedience for that forgiveness. But we all know of glaring exceptions, where unyielding disciples wrecked their own homes, and/or damaged the testimony of the church while providing plentiful fodder for potshots and criticisms against us. In truth, there are no perfect Christians, just like there are no perfect people, for "all have sinned and fall short of the glory of God."

Further, it may not be our moral lapses that play the biggest role in the stained reputation of the church. To the extent the church is leaving the impression that we look down our morally superior noses at the rest of the world, we invite its somewhat just criticism. But on atheism, it is hard to see how one person's morality is any different from someone else's. If, at length, morality is a human contrivance and wholly subjective, how can someone make an objective statement impugning the church or any other group? One man's immorality is another man's morality.

In some ways this statement is related to the one in chapter eleven, which insists that religion is a mental illness. It goes an additional step, however, claiming that our "illness" is hurting others, harming humanity with our judgmental, and hyper-critical attitudes. Fundamentally, committed Christians have the audacity to believe God's will is of primary importance. For us, it is supposed to trump all other considerations, and if the Christian worldview is true, we are right. Spoiler alert: The Christian worldview is true.

But many people in the world, not just atheists, have a different idea. They think how they *feel* about their lives, persuasions, and tendencies is of primary importance, and God and His commands and precepts are outdated suggestions. On that view, activities clearly prohibited by Scripture are not only permissible but sometimes celebrated. God commanded marital fidelity, but "He didn't know my husband." God commanded honesty, but "everybody" today needs to work a little "off the books" or "the government will eat you alive with taxes." Jesus' "render unto Caesar" *thing* did not anticipate life in 21st century America.

Some time ago I was counselling a young man who struggled with same-sex attraction. He was a singer in a Christian group, and he felt properly convicted and wanted freedom from his attendant besetting sin of the practice of homosexuality. He had "walked the aisle" many times, hoping that a deliverance prayer would do the trick and make his desires miraculously vanish—but to no avail.

On the view that our emotions are the barometer for whether something is morally appropriate, he should have had no problem. Why couldn't he just do what so many homosexuals do and justify his behavior because "God made me this way?" He would have been in good company, or at least he would have numerous people in agreement with him. But he was convinced, the One Who most mattered to him, the Lord God, could not be numbered among them. He had figured out something that eludes moral relativists and those who justify their own immoral behaviors; when I decide what is permissible for me, and redefine morality based on my preferences, I have done no damage to objective morality, but I am doing untold damage to myself and others. No matter what he told himself, or what society affirmed, an objective standard affirmed his primal urges as out of bounds—desires to be fought with, not embraced.

Still, the deliverance prayers did not appear to be effective, and he was at some loss to know what to try next. When he came to me, I decided to seek the counsel of an old college friend, Dennis Jernigan, who has a well-known testimony of identifying, earlier in his life, as a homosexual. I am paraphrasing the way that conversation went, from memory. The gist of it is accurate.

"Dennis," I asked, "How were you able to turn the corner and stop having the urges and put an end to lustful patterns?" I will probably never forget his response. "Jeff," he said, "When that happens, I will let you know. But for today, I am living this day, like I have every day of the past thirty-five years, faithful to my God, my wife, whom I adore, my children, grandchildren, and my testimony of faith in Christ." He continued, "The day when I do not have improper urges may never arrive, but by the grace of God I will live today like I have lived each of the others. If I was a problem drinker, most people would understand that I might always technically *be* an alcoholic—in recovery, sober, not drinking, but prone to that unproductive desire. I think all people have a besetting sin, something that Satan can use, if they are not on guard and diligent, to trip them up and cause untold damage. I know that's not necessarily the answer you wanted to hear, but I am happy with the Lord, and fulfilled in my life, marriage, and ministry and that is the truth of my experience."

That is an answer the world needs to hear and heed. The idea that it is somehow *progress* for people to stop struggling and working toward moral improvement, and instead to simply approve of, as moral, whatever activities they feel like doing, is leading to, and has led to some very serious social consequences. We can redefine what we *consider* moral, but we cannot erase the stain and consequences of crossing the boundaries God has set. Living with moral dissonance does serious harm to cultures and societies and destroys individuals. It is a soul-fracturing state, contributing to anxiety, and all manner of psychologically destructive conditions.

Clear lines are being drawn between the true, faithful church and culture. The church diametrically opposes the notion that we may simply redefine morality to suit our tastes and many in our culture seem strongly convinced that our beliefs are outmoded, out of date, out of style, and even harmful. Unfortunately, the social experiments that are testing which side is right may cause irreversible damage. The true church, rather than "doing harm" is actively fighting the harm inflicted by moral relativism. President George W. Bush was not referring to our decaying social climate when he referred to the "soft bigotry of low expectations," but the phrase certainly applies.

In summary, the humanitarian and social ministry of the church has been and continues to be positive. The church led the revolutions in public education, healthcare, the arts, and the sciences. The spiritual mission of the church has not been demonstrated to be errant and is more likely true than false. Additionally, the moral influence and ideals of the church are those that are likely to produce the greatest good on both personal and corporate levels. All of which refutes the notion that the church does more harm than good.

According to a Pew Research poll, "A majority of atheists (70%) in the United States say churches and other religious organizations do more harm than good in society."[61] This means that a strong majority of atheists, at least in the United States, are largely ignorant of the truth about this subject. But it also indicates that a sizeable minority, perhaps nearing 30%, may realize that the church is doing commendable work, even if they disagree with the fundamental reasons why churches pursue that work.

A helpful response, as always, should start with the question, "What makes you think that?" and/or "What evidence led you to think so?" Both those questions are diagnostic. There are lots of reasons, most of which we have touched on, and you should not borrow trouble by assuming one or more of their reasons and making an unnecessary defense. Once you know what you are dealing with, a gentle, respectful response can be made. Approach, as always, is important. One response may be to say, "I guess you know I disagree with that, but I can see where you are coming from. If I had the same information to go on, I might have come to the same conclusion. May I offer you some additional information and tell you why I see it differently?"

Agree where you can, correct where you can, and whatever you do, do not defend the indefensible. Neither should you feel the need to apologize for actions that are not your own. You might say something such as, "The church is certainly a large target, so I think we must talk about net positive or negatives, not individual instances I am sure we would both agree are egregious. Is that fair?" If your atheist friend does

[61] https://www.pewresearch.org/fact-tank/2019/12/06/10-facts-about-atheists/ retrieved 11/09/2022

not agree to a "reasonable" and fair conversation, they may not be ready to have a profitable discussion and you should probably bow out politely and tell them why.

At least in recent history, a much better case may be made that atheism has had a worse impact on humanity, by far, than the church has in its entire existence. In the twentieth century atheist despots and dictators, for example, were responsible for more mass murder, by magnitudes and orders of at least thousands, than leaders and members of any other movement in the history of the world.

I only mention that as an answer "in kind," not an accusation of atheists as a group. It would be just as wrong to throw every atheist into the category of murderer as it would be to indict all churches for the larceny, paedophilia, or other crimes of a few errant leaders. But in the aggregate, and in sheer numbers, based solely on actual statistics, a much more robust case that atheism is truly harmful can be made.

Despite repeated insistence to the contrary, there is no indication that churches, or belief in God, do *any* societal harm. If we are going by data, it is not even a case of the pot calling the kettle "black." It is practically a case of the pot claiming it is *not* a pot and blaming the kettle for any and every bad thing that gets cooked. For atheist to lob accusations at the church for perceived harm to culture or society takes a tone-deafness of the first order, and a complete lack of introspection. Yet despite overwhelming statistics demonstrating it is false, many atheists believe the mindlessly repeated mantra that religious belief is the world's greatest source of human conflict and violence. The irony is that atheism, not religion, is the worldview behind the most significant mass murders in history. Atheist thugs ranging from China's Chairman Mao, Premier Joseph Stalin of the former Soviet Union, Karl Marx, Pol Pot, Enver Hoxha, Ceaușescu, Fidel Castro to Kim Jong-Il performed the vilest acts and conducted the most vicious murderous rampages in all of history. Mao's regime, on its own, racked up a breathtaking seventy million deaths.[62] Cambodia's Pol Pot eliminated about one-fifth of its entire population.

When such data is cited, atheists respond in various ways. Richard Dawkins says, "What matters is. . . whether atheism systematically influences people to do bad things. There is not the smallest evidence that it does." He continues, "Individual atheists may do evil things but they don't do evil things *in the name of atheism*."[63] Fair enough, but the ideas derived from atheism—that mankind is nothing special, morality is wholly subjective, there is no final justice of judgment, and we are all products of an evolutionary system that rewards the fittest with survival and the less fit with extinction, fit hand in glove with dogmas that echo the sentiments of a great number of murderous regimes in recent history.

If we are treating atheism in the same way we insist the church must be treated, then it is hard to just let atheism off the hook. Something intrinsic to it appears to make powerful men bloodthirsty and to remove all restraint against immoral and despicable behaviors.

---

[62] Jung Chang and Jon Halliday, *Mao: The Unknown Story* (New York, NY: Knopf, 2005), 216.

[63] Richard Dawkins, *The God Delusion* (Boston, MA: Houghton Mifflin, 2006), 273, 279.

It seems a little too common to be chalked up to coincidence.

Invariably, if this part of the conversation arises, someone will bring up Hitler and claim that he was a Christian. They may go even further and say that his antisemitism was intrinsically connected to his Christian faith. He killed Jews because they were opposed to Christianity. There are at least two things they have gotten wrong about Hitler.

1. He killed Jews because he considered them to be racially, not religiously, inferior. A Jew could not escape the Gulag by claiming atheism or conversion to Christianity.

2. He was, by no means, a Christian, flatly stating that Christianity was one of the biggest "scourges" of history.

Of the "superior" German people he implored, "Let's be the only people who are immunized against this disease," and he suggested "through the peasantry we shall be able to destroy Christianity."[64]

When an atheist levels a critique asserting that Christianity is doing harm, the first step is determining what kind of "harm" to which they are referring. You should never go out of your way to answer a charge that is not being made. If they're generally critical because religious people are harmfully superstitious, or blatantly anti-science those are unwarranted assumptions that they cannot bear the burden of proving. If they have a moral issue with some Christians, then they

---

[64] Adolph Hitler, *Hitler's Table Talk 1941-1944: His Private Conversations* (New York, NY: Enigma Books, 2000).

cannot have it both ways.

If Christians (in general) are to be indicted for specific crimes committed by individual Christians, then atheism is fair game to blame for the crimes of atheist despots. Worse still, immoral Christians are working in ways that are *inconsistent* with their worldview, but the same thing may not be able to be said for an immoral atheist. There are, of course, a great number of moral atheists, as I have previously written, but on atheism, there is no ultimate truth or objective morality, only group and individual opinions.

In sincerity, God's church, His bride, is the hope of the world. We are bringing the truth of the gospel, which is the most important work for the good of humanity. We are pointing people to the One Who is the Way, the Truth, and the Life. Churches are far from perfect, but they are lightyears ahead of everything that trails them, especially atheism, which entails a wholesale denial of the witness of Christ, repudiation of the sovereignty of God, and has no foundation for objective morality. I *would* say "Atheism does more harm than good," but I cannot think of any *good* which atheism accomplishes.

Churches Do More Harm Than Good

1. What did you find helpful in this lesson?

2. Which part or parts of the lesson, if any, gave you pause?

3. Can you think of some ways that churches cause harm? What does the church, at large, need to change to better fulfill its mission?

4. This is the last session of this course work. Reflect on the semester. What are some of the most important concepts you considered together?

5. Do you have a desire to continue learning how to defend your faith and share it more powerfully and consistently with others? Why, or why not?

6. What experiences, if any, can you recall having with people who
   believe the statement that "churches do more harm than good?"

7. Would you have answered this complaint differently than the author? If so, how?

Share burdens, praises, concerns, and needs with one another and pray for one another.

Epilogue

These are Precious People

Have you hugged an atheist today? You would be surprised how effective true love and honest concern can be. There are, of course, exceptions, but as a group, atheists are better educated, more intelligent, and higher performing than the general population. They are your neighbors, co-workers, relatives, and friends. Like the other people in your community, they are (generally speaking) not anarchist, ill-tempered, inconsiderate, or rude. They are trying to raise considerate, industrious, honest children. They are diligent in their work ethic.

They are wrong about the most important thing, but they are not wrong about everything. They love faithfully, feel deeply, speak honestly (as they see it), laugh heartily, and play hard. They are people Christ loves so much He was willing to leave Heaven, become

---

incarnate in the womb of a young maiden in 1st century Palestine, live with us, and die with us. So, even when they think they are, no atheist is your enemy. And even if they were, our Master told us to *love* our enemies and *pray* for those who despitefully use us.

Satan wants us to have adversarial relationships with the people Christ wants us to befriend. Such people often have sincerely held beliefs that do not match our own. They are in the unenviable position of not knowing the One Who loves them most. Our sacred duty is to reflect Christ so often and so well that they become more open and receptive to *Him* through what they know of *us*. We are supposed to be Jesus with skin on. That means I love like He does, unconditionally, walk like He does, worthily and circumspectly, talk like He does— about the kingdom of God and His righteousness, and I keep His priorities as my own, to seek and to save that which is lost.

A word of caution: You might never feel fully prepared to share Christ with hard-core, militant unbelievers. They will likely ask questions you are not prepared to answer. Frequently, they are deeply entrenched in their rejection. They are often rude and dismissive. If you wait until you can handle all of that with relative composure and aplomb, you will never start some important conversations.

Those conversations are too important to put off until you know every answer by heart. No one is that fully prepared. But we all must start. We have been commissioned. So, what's a person to do? I've spent over four decades seeing atheists come to Christ. Here is my number one strategy. Ask God to give you an obvious, heart-felt, genuine love for all the people He died for. Love not only covers a multitude of sins, but it beats a path through stubborn hearts, despite strong opposition, defiance, and forceful pushback. Their fight is not (ultimately) with you, and their arms are too short to box with God.

When you love me, you can tell me I need a breath mint, or my fly is unzipped. When you love me, you earn the right to talk to me about sensitive subjects, and to confront me and challenge me when we disagree with one another. Atheists do not know it, but they need to be loved by us, . . . really loved. They need people to care enough about them to overlook the attitude, the defiance, their air of superiority and refusal to yield, and someone who will keep hoping all things, believing all things, and enduring all things. You are a likely candidate for the job because God rescued you and placed His Spirit within you.

Not only are you commissioned, but if you step out, as prepared as possible, in trust, you will discover He has empowered you for this purpose (Acts 1:8). Fully half the job of yielding to the Holy Spirit simply involves refusing to take over—to jump in and let your flesh give someone a "piece of your mind." Deep breathing, meditative reflection, calm demeanor, and growing dependence are all indicative of a Spirit-controlled witness. The words to the hymn come to mind, "I'm learning to lean, learning to lean, learning to lean on Jesus, finding more power than I've ever seen, I'm learning to lean on Jesus."

Our walk with Christ is a journey of discovery. Each day we walk fully aware of His presence brings new insight and more personal growth and development. Do not fear making some wrong assumptions and taking some wrong steps. Just be quick to apologize and always lead with love. Don't try to "best," or beat your friend. Atheists are not your opponents. If you love strongly you cannot fail. You will face rejection, just get used to the idea. People are not rejecting you, so refuse, no matter what they say, to take any of it personally. You're not responsible for anyone's reaction. You don't get the credit when someone repents, or the blame when they don't. That's not how it works. Be as cunning as a serpent and as gentle as a dove (Matthew 10:16). So far as it depends on you, be at peace with every person (Romans 12:18).

Despite the title of this book, Atheists are not the only ones who believe silly things. One of the silliest things a *Christian* may believe is that somehow, for any number of bogus reasons, they are *exempt* from participation in the "Great Commission" (Matthew 28:19, 20). If you are tempted to excuse yourself, you're being silly. The fields are white, . . . ready for harvest (John 4:35), and just like always, these "crops" come in many varieties, bearing many different labels. Different "crops" are harvested in different ways. Oranges aren't harvested like corn, but they both need to be harvested. Hardened atheists are not harvested like kids in Vacation Bible School, but He is still calling laborers into the harvest. For the King and His kingdom, do your part, nothing more, but certainly nothing less.

Never stop learning. "Be diligent to present yourself approved to God as a worker who does not need to be ashamed, accurately handling the word of truth" (2 Timothy 2:15). Develop a library of resources and set aside time—preferably daily—to study, read, think, and pray.

Share your faith every day. One of my dear mentors, Dr. Richard Hogue, indicated that witnessing is the greatest spiritual exercise and the most important spiritual discipline a Christian may practice. Although I heard him preach this principle over forty years ago, it is still vivid in my mind, and it drives me to this day.

According to Richard, that is because someone may read the word of God, even know the Bible well, yet become so "word-obsessed" that they neglect prayer and witnessing. The same thing can happen with a life that is focused on prayer. Prayer can become such an obsession that it forces other Christian disciplines to the side. It can become a goal, rather than a means to a goal. But witnessing is different. I may be able to do Bible study without praying and witnessing, and to pray while neglecting Bible study and sharing my faith, but if I take witnessing seriously, I will meet people and face circumstances that force me *into* the word and *onto* my knees.

I have noticed I witness more when I *plan* for it. When I build witnessing into my schedule and my daily plans, I often have additional *divine* appointments I was *not* planning for. When I do not, I rarely do. Two facts impact my witnessing more than anything else. Like you, I make time for what is important to me. Like you, I am a creature of habit. What is important to you? Who is important to you?

The late Francis Schaeffer wrote a lot of consequential books. The title of one of them, while it was not specifically about, or at least not limited to personal evangelism, is always on my mind as I think of the privilege of knowing and sharing the Lord Jesus. Francis Schaeffer asked, so pointedly, in light of what is true, Who we serve, what He commissioned, and a host of other relevant factors, "How should we then live?"[65] To all but the most stubbornly rebellious, the answer is obvious. "I have been crucified with Christ, and it is no longer I who live, but Christ lives in me; and the life which I now live in the flesh I live by faith in the Son of God, who loved me and gave Himself up for me." (Galatians 2:20).

---

[65] Francis Schaeffer, *How Should we Then Live? The Rise and Decline of Western Thought and Culture* (Wheaton IL: Crossway, 1976).

Bibliography

Bock, Darrell L. and Wallace, David B. *Dethroning Jesus.* Nashville, TN: Thomas Nelson, 2007.

Broocks, Rice. *God's Not Dead: Evidence for God in an Age of Uncertainty.* Edinburgh, Scotland: W. Publishing Group, 2013.

Cairnes, Earl E. *Christianity Through the Centuries: A History of the Christian Church.* Grand Rapids, MI: Zondervan Publishing House, 1996.

Carter, Robert, ed. *Evolution's Achilles' Heels.* Powder Springs, GA: Creation Book Publishers, 2015. (A young earth creationism perspective)

Chang, Jung and Halliday, Jon. *Mao: The Unknown Story.* New York, NY: Knopf, 2005.

Copan, Paul. *Is God a Moral Monster? Making Sense of the Old Testament God.* Grand Rapids, MI: Baker Books, 2011.

Copan, Paul and Meister, Chad, ed. *Philosophy of Religion: Classic and Contemporary Issues.* Malden, MA: Blackwell Publishing, 2008.

Craig, William Lane. *On Guard: Defending Your Faith with Reason and Precision.* Colorado Springs, CO: David C. Cook, 2010.

Craig, William Lane. *Reasonable Faith: Christian Truth and Apologetics.* Wheaton IL: Crossway, 2008.

Dawkins, Richard. *The God Delusion.* Boston, MA: Houghton Mifflin, 2006. (By a skeptical author)

Dawkins, Richard. *The Selfish Gene.* New York: Oxford University Press, 1989. (By a skeptical author)

Deere, Jack. *Surprised by the Power of the Spirit.* Grand Rapids, MI: Zondervan, 1993.

Dembski, William A., and Licona, Michael R. ed. *Evidence for God.* Grand Rapids, MI: Baker Books, 2010.

Dunn, James. *The Evidence for Jesus.* Louisville, KY: Westminster, 1985.

Ehrman, Bart. *Misquoting Jesus.* San Francisco, CA: Harper San Francisco, 2005. (By a skeptical author)

Erickson, Millard J. *Christian Theology.* Grand Rapids, MI: Baker Academic, 2013.

Geisler, Norman L. *Christian Apologetics.* Grand Rapids, MI: Baker Academic, 2013.

Geisler, Norman L. and Turek, Frank. *I Don't Have Enough Faith to Be an Atheist.* Wheaton, IL: Crossway, 2004.

Groothuis, Douglas. *Christian Apologetics: A Comprehensive Case for Biblical Faith.* Downers Grove, IL: IVP Academic, 2011.

Guillen, Michael. *Believing is Seeing: A Physicist Explains How Science Shattered His Atheism and Revealed the Necessity of Faith.* Carol Stream, IL: Tyndale Refresh, 2021.

Habermas, Gary and Licona, Michael R. *The Case for the Resurrection of Jesus.* Grand Rapids, MI: Kregel Publications, 2004.

Habermas, Gary. *The Risen Jesus and Future Hope.* Boulder, CO, New York, NY: Rowman and Littlefield Publishers, 2003.

Habermas, Gary. *The Verdict of History: Conclusive Evidence for the Life of Jesus.* Nashville, TN: Thomas Nelson, 1988.

Hamer, Dean. *The God Gene: How Faith Is Hardwired into Our Genes*. New York, NY: Anchor Books, 2005. (Not a "Christian" book)

Hannam, James. *The Genesis of Science: How the Christian Middle Ages Launched the Scientific Revolution*. Washington D.C.: Regnery Press, 2011.

Harris, Sam. *The End of Faith: Religion, Terror, and the Future of Reason*. New York, London: W. W. Norton and Company, 2004. (By a skeptical author)

Hitchens, Christopher. *God Is Not Great: How Religion Poisons Everything*. New York, NY: Twelve Books, 2007. (By a skeptical author)

Hitler, Adolph. *Hitler's Table Talk 1941-1944: His Private Conversations*. New York, NY: Enigma Books, 2000.

Miethe, Terry L., ed. *Did Jesus Rise from the Dead? The Resurrection Debate*, San Francisco: Harper and Row, 1987.

Moreland, J.P. *A Simple Guide to Experiencing Miracles:*

Instruction and Inspiration for Living Supernaturally in Christ. Grand Rapids, MI, Zondervan Reflective, 2021.

Moreland, J.P. and Craig, William Lane. *Philosophical Foundations for a Christian Worldview*. Downer's Grove, IL: IVP Academic, 2003.

Morley, Brian K. *Mapping Apologetics: Comparing Contemporary Approaches*. Downers Grove, IL: IVP Academic, 2015.

Morris, Henry M. *Science and the Bible*. Chicago, IL: Moody Press, 1986. (Dr. Morris was a young earth creationist)

Qureshi, Nabeel. *No God But One: Allah or Jesus?* Grand Rapids, MI: Zondervan, 2016.

Ratzsch, Del. *Science and Its Limits: The Natural Sciences in Christian Perspective.* Downers Grove, IL: IVP Academic, 2000.

Rhodes, Ron. *Answering the Objections of Atheists, Agnostics, & Skeptics.* Eugene, OR: Harvest House, 2006.

Richards, E Randolph and O'Brien, Brandon J. *Misreading Scripture with Western Eyes.* Downers Grove, IL, IVP Books, 2012.

Ross, Hugh and Kathy. *Always be Ready: A Call to Adventurous Faith.* Covina, CA: RTB Press, 2018. (Dr. Ross is an old earth creationist)

Ross, Hugh. *The Fingerprint of God.* Orange, CA: Promise Publishing, 1991.

Ross, Hugh. *Navigating Genesis: A Scientist's Journey through Genesis 1 – 11.* Covina, CA: RTB Press, 2014.

Schaeffer, Francis. *A Christian Manifesto.* Westchester, IL: Crossway Books, 1981.

Schaeffer, Francis. *How Should we Then Live? The Rise and Decline of Western Thought and Culture.* Wheaton IL: Crossway, 1976.

Stedman, Rick. *31 Surprising Reasons to Believe in God: How Superheroes, Art, Environmentalism, and Science Point Toward Faith.* Eugene, OR: Harvest House, 2017.

Taylor, Doug. *Why? A Believer's Introduction to Defending the Faith.* Nashville, TN: Westbow Press, 2015.

Wallace, J. Warner. *God's Crime Scene: A Cold-case Detective Examines the Evidence for a Divinely Created Universe.* Colorado Springs, CO: David C. Cook, 2015.

Wallace, J. Warner. *Person of Interest: Why Jesus Still Matters in a World That Rejects the Bible.* Grand Rapids, MI: Zondervan Reflective, 2021.

Whitcomb, John C. and Morris, Henry M. *The Genesis Flood: The Biblical Record and its Scientific Implications.* Phillipsburg, NJ: P&R Publishing, 1961, 2011. (Written from a young earth creationism perspective)

Appendix A

Conversation Seeds

With Friends

- I am a little embarrassed, but I've not checked up on you lately about your atheism. I know it's important to you, so please forgive me.

- I am a little embarrassed because we haven't talked in a while about your atheism. I don't want you to think I don't care. Considering what I believe, I would have to really dislike you not to at least try to get you to reconsider every so often.

- When something significant happens, of a spiritual nature: I know you're an atheist, but you're also my friend. Do you mind if I tell you something that happened that's neat?

- When you want to invite your friend to a special Christian opportunity: "Hey Wanda, if you don't mind hanging out with a bunch of Christians for 90 minutes (provide a close estimate of the time), Shirley is singing in the kid's choir on Sunday, and she would love it if you could come. Lunch is at our house after."

- Come over Friday night, we're all watching a movie. I've got to warn you, it's a Christian movie, but unlike most of them, I've heard this one is good.

- We're having a book club, and we're trying to have as many worldviews represented as possible. Are you still an atheist?*

---

* We have hosted "worldview groups," where the whole idea is to get to know each other deeply and share freely—no judgementalism and no arguing.

- Jim, I was thinking the other day, about you and your worldview. Does it bother you to talk about it with me?

- Betty, if you knew, or strongly suspected I was in danger would you tell me? Would you warn me even if I'd rather be in denial? Please understand, that's how I feel about you too.

With Neighbors

- Host a block party, mow their yard if it needs it, help carry groceries to their doorstep, take over some home-baked cookies, invite them over for game or movie night—i.e., find ways to turn neighbors into friends.

- Tell me about yourself. What's your name? Where did you grow up? What do you enjoy doing? Do you have children/grandchildren? People love talking about themselves, and (bonus) they open up to you when you're interested in them.

- If you discover your neighbor is a spiritual skeptic do not noticeably react to it, but secure permission to talk more about it from time to time. I would love to talk more about this sometime. Are you open to that? If they say, "No," there are other ways to influence people besides having a blatant and unwanted conversation. Start with a friendship and you may win the right to be heard.

- Strongly convey that you are truly interested in why they do not believe in God. Don't lie or indicate (in any way) that they may be able to change your mind, but assure them that you will not judge them, or think less of them, and you would love to have discussions (plural) with each other about why you believe as you (each) do.

- Let's get together for coffee and/or breakfast this Saturday. IMPORTANT: They have permitted you to talk about things that matter, so chit-chat a little, but also get down to business. If, after securing their permission, you still don't ask about their atheism and share your reasons for faith, you have not only blown an opportunity but possibly left the impression that Christ is not all that important to you. They do not know you are afraid or nervous.

- Most atheists, when asked what they will say if they die and discover they were wrong, say something such as, "I will ask God, 'Why didn't you make Yourself known?'" They place the onus on God as if He was unfair by lack of a more obvious, specific, undeniable revelation. Knowing that, ask the question like this: Just imagine with me that you die and discover you are wrong (use present tense). You hear God speak, and it's like the sound of mighty, rushing waters. He says, "I spoke to you plainly and clearly, reaching out to you to offer my love and acceptance, but you would not receive me." Is He lying? It does not matter how they reply. You are trying to start an open, transparent, substantive conversation, and this question is often helpful.

- Do you have any religious background? Are there any Christians in your family? What? Who? What do they say to you? Remember: Your goal is to break the ice and get conversation flowing. Be curious, kind, friendly—in other words display the fruit of the Spirit. If you get truly curious about your neighbor's background and story, not just to use it to win them, but to truly win a new friend you will be living the Christ kind of life.

- If you know that someone believes they "deconstructed" their faith and used to identify as a Christian, ask what data led to their change of heart? Ask if you can do a book swap with them— you'll read one they recommend, and they'll read one of yours. Read the one they provide—do your research on refuting it and meet to discuss your thoughts. Recommend a book that addresses their criticisms of Christianity.

With Relatives

Sometimes the hardest people to talk with are our own family members. Now and then they bring a dynamic to the table that can be threatening. Adult children may withhold visits with grandchildren from grandparents they think are too religious. All kinds of relationship blackmail overtones may be unspoken, but very much at play, especially between parents and kids. Some parents of atheists already feel guilty, thinking they've done something wrong, or their child would not be rejecting God. The reverse situation is also common; believing children have trouble talking to, especially disagreeing and/or correcting the people who loved and raised them and were always at the top of the relationship dynamic.

You must look for and pick your moments, when peace and love are ruling. When appropriate, leave breadcrumbs, and make gestures, subtle overtures of consistency, dependability, and faithfulness. Your loved one knows your beliefs, values, and commitments—and they should see those attributes on display as (more or less) a constant witness.

Practice your faith conspicuously, but not obnoxiously. For example, when you are in a home which does not pray, you should usually not ask to lead a prayer before their meal, but you could bow briefly and silently offer your own prayer before lifting it to say, "Please pass the potatoes." [Be consistent: If you don't bless every meal in your own home but you make a show in public this little hypocrisy will likely not be lost on your relative and will serve to reinforce their negative view(s) of Christians.]

You will find your conversations along the way, as you incline your spiritual ear to the Spirit and keep yourself tuned and ready. And, along the way, be the best relative, most dependable, fun, loving husband, brother, dad, sister, mom you can be. You would think you should not need to *earn* the right to be heard by someone you literally nursed, changed, and sheltered to adulthood, but family works that way. Perhaps you are feeling just a little of how God must feel.

Above all, never stop praying, and never stop growing. Be quick to make amends and live fully present in the moments you are with your unsaved relative. Be available and close when they are ready to talk, make a change, and perhaps surrender.

With Associates

Many of the same "seeds" you use to start conversations with a friend may also be used with associates. Our "work friends" aren't necessarily the people we hang with after hours, but there's no reason they shouldn't be. We spend half our waking hours on the mission field of our job.

- Dude, we're having a game night at the house. What are you doing Friday night? How about the next week?

- Sheila, I'm hosting a shower for Mary and her fiancé. Do you think you could come? [If you both know Mary, and you are hosting the party, there is no reason why you cannot pray for the couple, and on your turf a wedding or baby shower can have many distinctively Christian aspects.]

- If your associate brings up their spiritual point of view you might say, "I know we don't have time at work. Even though we don't see eye to eye I want to talk to you some more about that. Let's go for a coffee." When you are up front about your intentions your associate will not feel used or blindsided. Make sure you follow up and go for coffee/soda/pie, and you pick up the tab. Talk is cheap, but you shouldn't be.

- When you think you know someone's position based on something they have said that's pejorative, either about religion, church, or God, make sure you clarify. Sometimes people speak the way they think is "work appropriate," because they are too weak to stand up for larger principles and convictions they keep buried and/or well-hidden. I have met many people who have a background of Christianity and do not deny the reality of God, who nevertheless have a social stance that is more defiant than their actual feelings. You might create a safe space for them to have someone at work with whom to "work out" their objections.

- Many atheists see themselves as broad-minded and unperturbed by disagreements about faith. Others find the subject nauseating. Some are on a mission to make the whole world see things the way they do. Finding out which kind of atheist you are talking with is not difficult. Just ask. "I know some people can be touchy about the subject and don't want anyone trying to change their mind. Are you pretty sure of what you (don't) believe?" If you are speaking to an "atheism evangelist" they will be excited that you asked.

- Be thoughtful and considerate. It's hard to dislike someone who likes you. They may question your taste, but they will almost always like you back.

Workplace evangelism is a sensitive subject. Your employer has a right to expect that your soulwinning efforts take a backseat to your excellent job performance. As a Christian, you should be performing all your tasks as "unto the Lord." Be scrupulous and attentive to see that your evangelism efforts neither distract from nor interfere with a productive environment. Make it your goal to earn the respect and win the ear of the people you work with. Stay positive, productive, and present in your performance and in your work relationships.

At work, if someone asks you *not* to speak with them about your faith you must respect their wishes. If you don't, you may violate harassment laws. Consider how you would feel if the shoe was on the other foot, and a Satanist just would not (from your perspective) leave you alone. Instead, concentrate on building a friendship. Admittedly, however, when someone is already "on alert" about you this (building a friendship) may not be possible. Sometimes you must hand off the ball, i.e., change strategies. Perhaps another Christian will be open to investing time to build a friendship. Sadly, it is often hard to find another Christian who is actively sharing his/her faith.

The number one Bible verse for workplace witnessing is Romans 12:18, "If possible, so far as it depends on you, be at peace with all people." Don't take this to an extreme and be someone who doesn't stand for truth, justice, and equity. The first two words, "If possible" suggest that there will be times when conflict is unavoidable. Someone running from God resists His ambassadors. A militant, sinful crowd shouted, "Crucify Him," and "Give us Barabbas!" Some people, who are angry with God, will lash out at you. If Jesus couldn't please everyone, neither will you. "Just keep doin' your best, pray that it's blessed" and let Him "take care of the rest."[66]

Staying quiet is not an option. There is far too much at stake. Atheists currently in your life, and those you will meet, have likely had plenty of experience with quiet, fear-filled Christians. In most cases, at least in this country, if properly approached, at the right time, and under the right conditions, they love talking about the myriad reasons they don't believe. They know they are in a minority position, and they usually feel somewhat persecuted, but love to revel in their counter-cultural rebellion.

They would love to convince you that stereotypes of mean-spirited, angry atheists are wrong. You can use this to your advantage because their enterprise coincides with yours, to be civil, friendly, open, and accepted (or at least acceptable). They may have immediate, or extended family who they feel reject them, and they are often looking for a Christian representative to understand them, or even a Christian who will listen.

Despite these desires, the conviction of the Holy Spirit may make them irritable, and/or easily triggered (agitated), especially if you forget to speak gently and with respect (1 Peter 3:15). As their worldview collides with reality you can anticipate and expect some angst to follow; so be prepared to be supportive, kind, friendly, and calm, however they respond.

---

[66] Keith Green, "He'll Take Care of The Rest" Sparrow Records, 1977.

Appendix B
Helpful Web Addresses

- Acts17.org -This is the website of the ministry of Philosopher Dr. David Wood, a former atheist and brilliant defender of the faith, especially to Muslims.

- AnswersinGenesis.org – This is the web presence of a ministry headed by Young Earth Creationist and Founder of *The Ark Encounter*, Ken Ham. Young Earth Astronomer, Dr. Danny Faulkner, also blogs from this site.

- ApologeticsGuy.com - Mikel Del Rosario is an Apologetics Professor who also runs a helpful and fairly robust apologetics website.

- Apologetics315.com – "Apologetics 315 is a place where you can get daily apologetics resources including debates, podcasts, book reviews, quotes, and more."

- BraxtonHunter.com -Dr. Braxton Hunter, the President of Trinity Theological Seminary, uses apologetics effectively and seamlessly when presenting the gospel, as an Evangelist. His site features effective and helpful resources.

- CARM.org -Home to Matt Slick's *Christian Apologetics and Research Ministry*, this is one of the most comprehensive sites on the web, with thousands of searchable articles on various topics of interest.

- ColdCaseChristianity.com – This site is the web presence for Apologist and Cold Case Detective J. Warner Wallace.

- CrossExamined.org – This site features teaching from its founder, Dr. Frank Turek, on apologetics topics through a blog, social media, videos, training, and more.
- DouglasGroothuis.com – Dr. Groothuis has several useful resources and articles on his site.
- ICR.org – This is the web presence of the Young Earth organization founded by Dr. Henry M. Morris, The Institute for Creation Research.
- NGIM.org -This website features the ministry resources of the late Dr. Norman Geisler and the resources of his son, David Geisler. This site is especially good for those learning to integrate apologetics with evangelism and discipleship.
- ThePoachedEgg.net – This comprehensive site features over 10,000 articles by various Christian Apologists.
- ReasonableFaith.org -This is the website for the ministry founded by the brilliant Apologist, Theologian, and Philosopher, Dr. William Lane Craig.
- Reasons.org – This is the web presence of the Science apologetics ministry founded by Old Earth Creationist and astronomer, Dr. Hugh Ross.
- SeanMcDowell.org -The web presence of Biola Professor, Apologist, Philosopher, Sean McDowell.
- STR.org – Greg Koukl, Author of *Tactics*, Blogger, Podcaster, and Speaker leads a wonderful group of Christian thinkers, who all publish and produce helpful materials.

ABOUT THE AUTHOR

Dr. Jeff Payne is a sinful, finite, broken man, saved by the grace of God, but he does have a personalized Bible with his name engraved in gold (colored) leaf on the front cover. He is also, according to him, "educated far beyond" his intelligence.

Jeff and his wife, Kathleen, have been serving together in ministry since 1980, and Jeff started his ministry career in October of 1977. He is a lifelong learner, with the help, so far, of Oklahoma Baptist University, Liberty Home Bible Institute, Trinity Seminary, Dallas Theological Seminary, Cedarville University, Christian Bible College, Luther Rice Seminary, and Andersonville Seminary, culminating in three earned graduate degrees.

He serves as a Senior Pastor and is a Theologian, Philosopher, Apologist, Author, Teacher, Missionary Evangelist, and Psalmist. The churches he served set numerous national evangelism and baptismal records.

In addition to teaching and pastoring he is often available to speak in churches and other venues throughout the world.

Contact him via Email: cccbmt@gmail.com

Made in the USA
Columbia, SC
15 March 2024

32847654R00113